S0-BOE-787

JAMES PETIGRU BOYCE

SELECTED WRITINGS

TIMOTHY GEORGE

BROADMAN PRESS
Nashville, Tennessee

© Copyright 1989 • Broadman Press

All rights reserved

4265-90

ISBN: 0-8054-6590-1

Dewey Decimal Classification: 230

Subject Heading: THEOLOGY // BOYCE, JAMES PETIGRU

Library of Congress Catalog Card Number: 88-22976

Printed in the United States of America

Library of Congress Cataloging-in-Publication Data

Boyce, James Petigru, d. 1888.
  [Selections. 1989]
  James Petigru Boyce : selected writings / edited by Timothy
George.
    p. cm.
  Bibliography: p.
  ISBN 0-8054-6590-1
  1. Southern Baptist Convention—Doctrines. 2. Baptists-
Doctrines. 3. Southern Baptist Convention—Sermons. 4. Baptists-
Sermons. 5. Sermons, American. I. George, Timothy. II. Title.
BX6462.7.B692 1989
286'.132—dc19   88-22976

In piam memoriam

James Petigru Boyce	(1827 - 1888)
John A. Broadus	(1827 - 1895)
Basil Manly, Jr.	(1825 - 1892)
William Williams	(1821 - 1877)

Preface

A mere one hundred years after his death in 1888, James Petrigru Boyce has become the object of what might well be called "affectionate obscurity." Revered as the founder and first president of The Southern Baptist Theological Seminary, Boyce was also a formidable theologian and an influential denominational leader. He served nine terms as president of the Southern Baptist Convention! In a time of denominational ferment and theological controversy, we do well to look again at this major figure from our past. Of course, Boyce cannot be uprooted from his nineteenth-century setting and brought into our own context without remainder, but his courage, his struggles and his faith, his vision for theological education and his commitment to the great principles of historic Christian orthodoxy still stand as much needed guideposts for all who continue to "press toward the mark for the prize of the high calling of God in Christ Jesus."

The introductory essay in this volume was originally presented as the Founder's Day address in the Alumni Chapel of The Southern Baptist Theological Seminary on February 2, 1988. This service marked the one hundredth anniversary of the death of James Petrigru Boyce who died in southern France on December 28, 1888. The fullest biographical sketch of Boyce remains the *Memoir* which John A. Broadus, his lifelong friend and successor as president of the seminary, published in 1893. While the Broadus volume has served its readers well, the time is long overdue for a modern critical biography of Boyce whose life was a veritable prism into the currents of theology and church history, North and South, from the pre-Civil War period through the days of Reconstruction. The essay printed here is a thematic interpretation of Boyce's life and legacy which suggests several avenues for further research. Boyce's correspondence could well fill a separate volume of hefty size. Boyce and Broadus maintained a steady correspondence which is yet to be cataloged and critically edited. These letters, a few of which were printed in A. T. Robertson's *Life and Letters of John A. Broadus* (1901), are a rich source for understanding these two great Baptist leaders and the history of the seminary and the denomination to which they were devoted.

The second section of this volume reproduces Boyce's famous inaugural lecture at Furman University on "Three Changes in Theological Institutions." This address was described by Broadus as "epoch-making in the history of theological education among Southern Baptists." It was delivered on July 30, 1856, before the trustees of Furman University. A. M. Poindexter, secretary of the Foreign Mission Board, who was present on this occasion, claimed that this address was "the ablest thing of the kind he had ever heard." Boyce's triad of "changes" were revolutionary in the context of nineteenth-century ideals for theological education. He called for *openness* —a seminary for everybody called by God regardless of prior academic training; *excellence*—a course of instruction second to none in high scholarly standards; *confessional integrity*—a statement of doctrinal principles which every professor would heartily embrace and in accordance with which he would teach. This address proved to be the catalyst in the formation and organization of The Southern Baptist Theological Seminary which held its first session in the fall of 1859.

Francis Wayland, venerable Baptist educator under whom Boyce had studied at Brown University, gave the following assessment of the new plan for ministerial training.

> My dear Professor Boyce—I have read with great interest your Inaugural Address. It is the first common sense discourse on theological education I have yet seen. I like it for several reasons. In the first place, it does not take it for granted that the Theological Seminary is a stereotyped institution from which nothing is to be taken and to which nothing is to be added in all coming time; in the next place, it takes it for granted that a seminary is made for the church and not that the church was created by Christ for the seminary and especially for the professors. . . . I wish you every success. I hope you will be well sustained, and that Baptists, as they have done before, may show other Christians how the church of Christ is to be built up by following more closely in the steps of the Master. (Letter of January 26, 1857).

This edition of the "Three Changes" is the first complete reprinting since the original publication in Greenville, South Carolina, in 1856. A brief excerpt from the address was included in Robert A. Baker's *A Baptist Source Book* (1966).

Boyce's *magnum opus* was his *Abstract of Systematic Theology,* first published in 1882. This book, slightly revised by F. H. Kerfoot in 1899, was used for thirty-five consecutive years as the standard textbook in systematic theology at Southern Seminary. It was displaced only by E. Y. Mullins's *The Christian Religion in Its Doctrinal Expression* (1917) which in turn was dedicated to the memory of Boyce—"great administrator and teacher of theology, whose inspiring vision of theological education for Southern Baptists made possible The Southern Baptist Theological Seminary." A contemporary review of the *Abstract* commended the volume and described Boyce as "conservative and eminently Scriptural. He treats with great fairness those whose views upon various points discussed he declines to accept, yet in his own teaching, is decidedly Calvinistic, after the model of 'the old divines.' " In recent years Boyce's *Abstract* has been reprinted and widely distributed by a group of Southern Baptists who are committed to the Reformed theological perspective it embodies. This revival of interest in Boyce as a theologian is a healthy development. However, Boyce's theology was never intended to be relegated to the classroom or exhausted in a textbook. Boyce would have agreed with the Puritan divine William Ames who defined theology as "the science of living to God." Boyce was preeminently a churchman for whom piety and intellect, theology and spirituality were not polar opposites but rather discrete dimensions of a holistic Christian faith. The place where these emphases were most effectively integrated by Boyce was preaching. For this reason we have chosen to complete this anthology with a selection of Boyce's sermons.

In his survey of Boyce's writings, Broadus declared that "a volume ought to be published of Dr. Boyce's sermons and lectures." He then listed and described briefly ten of Boyce's sermons some of which he had heard preached and whose appeal he witnessed. A few of Boyce's sermons were privately printed during his lifetime, but most remained in manuscript form. For a number of years after Boyce's death, his sermon manuscripts were lost. The memory of his preaching, however, was kept alive by oral tradition, as the following letter of February 14, 1931, from the librarian at Southern Seminary to Boyce's daughter Elizabeth indicates:

> From time to time references are made in the classroom to your father's memorable sermon on the text, "In the beginning God," and I have repeated calls for it in the Library. I, myself, have often wished to read it but have never heard of its being in print, and I am turning to you to know if you can give us any information as to how we may obtain a copy of it. If we could even get the manuscript and make a copy we would be delighted to do so.

After considerable searching, a volume of Boyce's sermon manuscripts was discovered and presented to the seminary. Written in his own delicate hand, these sermons had been sewn together in a brown-backed binder and stored anonymously among miscellaneous items in a large warehouse. Several of the sermons included in this volume have been transcribed from these recovered manuscripts. They are published here for the first time.

The eight sermons published in this volume represent a small sampling of Boyce's vast homiletical output. They cover, however, a wide range of occasions and subjects and convey a sense of the versatility and breadth of Boyce's preaching style. The sermon, "In the Beginning God," already referred to, reflects the decidedly theocentric emphasis of Boyce's theology and shows his ability to blend poetic metaphor and logical discourse. "Thus Saith the Lord" was an ordination sermon Boyce preached for one of his former students, H. M. Wharton, upon his call as pastor of the First Baptist Church of Eufaula, Alabama. "Christ Receiving and Eating with Sinners" was described by Broadus as one of Boyce's "most delightful practical sermons. . . . The difference in color of the light thrown by the three illustrations [i.e. the parables of the lost sheep, the lost coin and the lost son] was depicted with delicate taste and deep feeling . . . the practical impression was wholesome and powerful." "The Place and Power of Prayer" was probably Boyce's most popular sermon. He repeated it in numerous churches upon special request. Together with "The Prayers of Christ," it shows Boyce's devotion to the spiritual life and his desire to foster a genuine piety amongst his hearers. "A Christmas Sermon to Children" is a delightful presentation of the gospel message to little ones. It demonstrates the ability of Boyce, the great theologian, to present the deepest mystery of the faith to the simplest members of his congregation. "The Uses and Doctrine of the Sanctuary" was a sermon preached at the dedication of a new house of worship in Columbia, South Carolina, at a church Boyce himself had earlier served as pastor. "Life and Death the Christian's Portion" is one of the few sermons Boyce had printed during his own lifetime. It was the funeral sermon for Basil Manly, Sr., friend and colleague. In the original published edition of this sermon, Boyce appended a lengthy biographical sketch of Manly, Sr., who had been his own boyhood pastor and mentor and who later served as the first chairman of the board of trustees of the seminary.

I wish to thank several persons without whose help this book would not have been published. President Roy L. Honeycutt encouraged my interest in Boyce and invited me to deliver the Founder's Day address on him. He also supported my work with the Boyce manuscripts and made possible the publication of this volume. Paulette Moore, seminary archivist, was an indefatigable helper in securing and reproducing materials by and about Boyce. Mark Dever brought to my attention many relevant documents and shared an enthusiasm for this project which inspired me to see it through to completion. John Hammett provided expert editorial assistance in the final stages of preparing the manuscript for press. Jackie Morcom helped to decipher near illegible passages in Boyce's handwriting and ably typed several drafts of the manuscript.

F. H. Kerfoot, who studied with Boyce and succeeded him as professor of systematic theology, once described his great teacher and mentor as "by birth and training a gentleman, by the grace of God a Christian, courtly and courteous in bearing, strong in convictions, chivalrous and dauntless in courage, wise and safe in counsel . . . The people trusted him and followed where he led. And now when they see him no more, they cannot follow a safer human leader in the outlining of their theological thought." This volume is dedicated to the memory of Boyce and the three men who served with him as the original founding fathers of Southern Seminary. They are without doubt among the greatest leaders that Southern Baptists have ever had. May their courage, commitment, and vision inspire us to remain faithful to the ideals for which they expended their lives, and in so doing remain faithful to Jesus Christ, their Lord and ours.

Contents

I

"Soli Deo Gloria! The Life and Legacy of James Petigru Boyce"

"Soli Deo Gloria! The Life and Legacy of James Petigru Boyce"*

On August 31, 1877, Southern Seminary opened its first session in Louis-ville, Kentucky. To some it seemed an inauspicious start for the fledgling seminary recently removed from Greenville, South Carolina. There were fewer than ninety students, only four faculty members—forced to hold classes in a rented building. Yet none of this was reflected in the words of James Petigru Boyce. Nearly six feet tall and weighing over two hundred pounds, he commanded great respect as he spoke to the faculty, students and friends of the seminary who had gathered that evening at the Walnut Street Baptist Church.

> We claim not yet to have attained the goal at which we aim; we are still pressing forward; yet not amid circumstances which call us to forget the past, but the rather to remember the days of old and to thank God and take courage .... Let the history, when written, tell only of the toils and trials and sacrifices and wisdom and prudence and foresight and prayers and tears and faith of the people of God, to whom it will have owed its existence and its possibilities of blessing. And God grant that it may go down to succeeding ages to bless His cause and glorify His name when all of us here have been forgotten in this world forever.[1]

Today, one hundred years after the death of Boyce, all of those who were present on that occasion have long since departed from this world forever. And yet it is appropriate that we remember them—and him—that we remember, as he said, "the days of old and thank God and take courage." We do so not merely as an exercise in hagiography, nor to indulge our fancy for nostalgia, but because of all of us who are a part of this seminary are also a part of Boyce and the other founders. We are covenant-partners with them in a great community of learning and piety, a community which lives, to be sure, amidst the ambiguities of history, but which is rooted ultimately in the purposes of God in eternity.

There was a time when Founder's Day addresses were delivered by aged alumni, men—they were all men in those days—who had studied with the great founders themselves and could recall personal anecdotes about them. The last Founder's Day address on Boyce was given in 1924. On that occasion, David Ramsey spoke of Boyce's "twinkling face," his great sense of humor. He told of E. C. Dargan, later a member of the seminary faculty, who said to Boyce at his commencement, "Doctor, I am sorry I am graduating without ever having sat in your class." Boyce replied, "That may be very well for you, for you might not have graduated if you had."[2] In those days students had nicknames for the professors. A. T. Robertson was "Dr. Bob." Sampey was "Tiglath," Mullins, "the Pope." Boyce's nickname was "Jim Peter," a term the students used behind his back but never to his face. Ramsey told of how Boyce with his own hands carried food from his elegant home to students who were sick; of how when typhoid fever was raging in Louisville Boyce would visit the stricken students and pray with them. In 1884, a second-year student named John R. Sampey, wrote in his diary: "Dr. Boyce was in good humor today, jesting with the professors. He is a grand man, a kindhearted Christian . . . I have learned to love Dr. Boyce."[3]

Over the years, however, Boyce has become the object of what might well be called "affectionate obscurity." He seems so distant, so far away. In 1950 President Ellis Fuller, in a letter to Miss Lucy Boyce, the last surviving daughter of the Boyce family, wrote, "We must wake up Boyce's name and put it upon the lips of students and faculty members because of what the name has meant, means now, and will continue to mean to Baptists throughout the world."[4] It is that spirit which has informed my own approach to Boyce. I present him to you not as an artifact from the past, but as a living, dynamic Christian, theologian, denominational leader, seminary founder, a forebearer in the faith, whom I too have learned to love. I have entitled this address, *"Soli Deo Gloria!"* "To God Alone Be the Glory!" for this, above all else, was the theme of the life and labors of James Petigru Boyce. We shall look first at Boyce's early life and his unique role in the founding of the seminary, then at his service as theologian and churchman, and finally we shall make some concluding remarks about his legacy which we have inherited and are charged to pass on to those who shall come after us.

Formation and Vocation

James Petigru Boyce was born on January 11, 1827 in Charleston, South Carolina. John C. Calhoun was vice-president of the United States, and Andrew Jackson was preparing to run for the White House. In 1827 the colony of Liberia was founded for the repatriation of American slaves. The

Erie Canal was two years old, and for ten years steamboats had made regular passage between New Orleans and Louisville. Charles Finney was creating a sensation with his "new measures" of revivalism. William Carey was still laboring in India, and Adoniram Judson in Burma. J. R. Graves was a lad of seven, and Robert E. Lee was a dashing cadet of twenty at West Point Academy.

Charleston, a city of thirty thousand, was a flourishing center of commerce and culture where two ideals of civilization converged: the Cavalier and the Puritan. The spirit of the jolly Cavalier, brought over from France and England, exemplified in fox hunting parsons and state-sponsored Anglicanism, resulted in a culture of civility and urbanity which left its imprint on young Boyce. His father Ker Boyce was the wealthiest man in South Carolina. A banker and business magnate, he desired his precious son to follow in his steps. Like the father of Martin Luther centuries before, Boyce's father had wanted his son to study law and was bitterly disappointed when he opted for the ministry instead. One of his father's business partners, upon hearing that Jimmy Boyce meant to be a preacher, said: "Well, well, why don't he follow some useful occupation."[5] Although he was to pursue a different path, Boyce did inherit his father's penchant for business success. He served as treasurer and financial agent of the seminary as well as chairman of the faculty and professor of theology. Without his extraordinary acumen in business and financial affairs, the seminary could not have survived.

The Cavalier culture is also reflected in Boyce's marked concern about manners. David Ramsey entitled his Founder's Day address on Boyce, "God's Gentlemen." At the seminary Boyce taught the students not only about justification and the eternal decrees of God but also how to eat properly with a fork and knife, how to help a lady into her seat, how to stand in a pulpit, how to dress correctly for class, how to make pastoral visits with propriety and discretion. It is not surprising, then, that Boyce shows up on Brooks Holifield's list of "gentlemen theologians" who had a decisive effect on Southern culture in the nineteenth century.[6]

However, it was not the Cavalier but the Puritan ideal which was to shape Boyce's destiny. His mother, descended from strict Presbyterian stock, was converted under the ministry of Basil Manly, Sr., who had come to be pastor of the First Baptist Church of Charleston in 1826. Boyce came under the tutelage of this great Baptist leader who was both an able exponent of the doctrines of grace and one of the earliest proponents of a common theological seminary for Southern Baptists. He was to serve as the chairman of the first board of trustees of Southern Seminary. Boyce later recalled the influence Manly, Sr., had on his young life: "I can yet feel the weight of his hand, resting in gentleness and love upon my head. I can recall the words of fatherly tenderness, with which he sought to guide my childish steps."[7] From his mother and from his pastor, Boyce gained a sense of the transcendent. He became attuned to the life of the spirit and the life of the mind. His "barrell-shaped" figure, as one of his contemporaries described him, prevented him from engaging in the popular schoolboy sports, such as baseball or shinny.

So far as I can tell, the only sport in which he excelled was archery, which does not require a great amount of physical exertion. More often, he was sequestered in a corner reading a book. Throughout his entire life, he was an omnivorous reader and a bibliophile without peer. Boyce was far from a recluse, however. He found time to waltz with the young ladies, one of whom described him as a very fine specimen of "episcopal dimensions," and to play practical jokes on his friends. One day after pulling some caper, he ran behind a tree which was not quite big enough to hide him. One of his teachers looking out of a window, said, "There is Boyce, who will be a great man, if he does not become a devil."[8]

After studying for two years at the College of Charleston, Boyce moved to Providence, Rhode Island, where he enrolled at Brown University, the first college founded by the Baptists in America. When Boyce arrived its president was Francis Wayland, renowned Baptist statesman and educator, one of the formative leaders of the Triennial Convention. Wayland had a great influence on Boyce in two ways. First, Boyce learned from Wayland the method of teaching by recitation. The student was required to memorize a given lesson in advance and stand to recite it when called upon in class. John R. Sampey gives us a glimpse of how this method actually worked. One day he came to Dr. Boyce's theology class unprepared to recite from the Latin text they had been assigned, but thinking he could "fake it" if called upon. He was called upon right away and found himself struggling over a difficult passage. Boyce helped him along at first, but then realized he was trying to recite without having prepared, Sampey says "he stuck his pencil to his lips and let me flounder for a minute or two, then called on another . . ." After class Sampey went forth to apologize. "You certainly owe me an apology," said Boyce. "I know I do, and I am making it the best I know how. I hope you will forgive me." Boyce studied a moment and said, "Yes, I will forgive you Sampey."[9] The next year Boyce added Sampey to the faculty. I'm not sure what lesson there is in that. The recitation method was used in some form at Southern Seminary until the 1940s, when Dr. Dale Moody introduced the more popular lecture format.

It was also under the influence of Francis Wayland that Boyce was converted to Christ. The Second Great Awakening had begun with a powerful revival at Yale College under Timothy Dwight. A similar outpouring of the Spirit occurred at Brown when Boyce was a student there. Dr. Wayland prayed for the students who had never professed faith in Christ and preached in chapel on the importance of spiritual welfare as well as intellectual advance. When Boyce returned to Charleston for spring break, he was under deep conviction. Despite his wealthy status, his promising future, his polish and education, Broadus says "he felt himself a ruined sinner and . . . had to look to the merits of Christ alone for salvation."[10] He was saved and baptized during a protracted meeting conducted by Richard Fuller.

When he returned to Brown, Boyce threw himself into his studies with renewed vigor. "I have laid out about three or four thousand pages to read," he wrote. "First there is Plato, then Mill's Logic; then the Republic of Letters; while on the moral and religious side come Wayland's Discourses, Milton's Paradise Lost, Bunyan's Pilgrim Progress, interspersed with other books occasionally." These were not textbooks, mind you; this was reading which he did on the side, as it were. At the same time, he became greatly concerned for his fellow classmates who were as yet unconverted. He began to pray for them and to share the gospel with them. "Two or three," he wrote, "who had been brought up in the doctrines of Universalism [came] to look to Jesus as the author and finisher of our faith." Again, he wrote, "May God make me instrumental in his hands in the salvation of many!" Both of these quotations, about his wide reading and his concern for the lost, are from the same letter. They point to one of the unifying themes of his life and legacy: the coinherence of intellect and piety. From his conversion in 1845 until his death in 1888, Boyce lost neither his devotion to God nor his dedication to disciplined study which was for him an expression of devotion to God.

Boyce received his formal theological training at Princeton Seminary where he studied from 1849 to 1851 under Archibald Alexander, his son Addison Alexander and—above all—Charles Hodge, whose three-volume *Systematic Theology* Boyce would later use as a textbook in his own classes. Robert Lynn has suggested that of the major theological seminaries in American Southern and Princeton are the closest in perspective, organization and intent. Both Southern and Princeton, he observed, are servants of a powerful denomination, each one is committed to doctrinal standards, and both enjoyed the advantage of a potent and long-lasting first generation of faculty members in their formative years. In accounting for this parallel development, we cannot ignore the fact that two of Southern's original founders, Boyce and Manly, Jr., were trained for their life's work at Princeton.

Boyce and Southern Seminary

After completing his work at Princeton, Boyce served for two years as pastor of the First Baptist Church of Columbia, South Carolina. At his ordination council, someone asked Boyce whether he proposed to make a life-long matter of preaching. "Yes," he replied, "provided I do not become a professor of theology."[11] In 1855, Boyce was elected to teach theology at Furman University. In July 1856, he delivered his inaugural address, entitled "Three Changes in Theological Institutions." One person who heard it said it was the most remarkable speech he had heard in his life. It is even more remarkable when you consider that it was delivered by a young man only twenty-nine years old. Every student at Southern Seminary should read and study this document. It is our declaration of independence. Its basic ideas were incorporated into the Fundamental Laws of the seminary and have served as the basis of our institutional life for 130 years.

Boyce's address was a virtual manifesto for a common theological seminary for Baptists in the South. He suggested three ideals which such a school should embody. The first was *openness*, a seminary for everybody called by God regardless of academic background or social status. This was unheard of in the nineteenth century when it was universally agreed that a thorough grounding in the classical disciplines was an essential prerequisite for theological education. Boyce had two concerns in proposing this change. First, he knew that the majority of Baptist preachers did not have, and many could not acquire, the advantages of a classical education, yet they and the churches they served would be enhanced by their exposure to theological study. He also hoped that the experience of students from diverse backgrounds mingling together in a common community of learning and piety would engender mutual respect and lessen the jealousies and resentments which frequently flared up among Baptist pastors—a phenomenon not entirely absent from contemporary church life.

His second ideal was equally important—*excellence*. Boyce was intent upon establishing an advanced program of theological study which in its academic rigor would be on a par with the kind of instruction offered at Princeton, Andover, Harvard, Yale or anywhere else in the world. He envisioned, as he put it, "a band of scholars," trained for original research, committed to accurate scholarship which would go out from the seminary to contribute significantly to the theological life of the church by their teaching and writing as well as by their preaching and witness in the world.

The third ideal was *confessional identity*. Boyce proposed that the seminary be established on a set of doctrinal principles which would provide consistency and direction for the future. This, too, was a radical step in the context of nineteenth-century Baptist life. Newton Theological Institute, the first seminary founded by Baptists in America, had no such confessional guidelines. Nor, indeed, did the Southern Baptist Convention, organized in 1845. The Abstract of Principles was Southern Baptists' first and, in my opinion, best confessional document. It was necessary, Boyce felt, to protect the seminary from dangers both the right and on the left. From his student days in New England, Boyce was aware of the recent currents in theology: Unitarianism, Transcendentalism, the New Divinity. In particular, he spoke against the "blasphemous doctrines" of Theodore Parker, who had denied that Christianity was based on a special revelation of God. At the same time he was concerned about populist theologies in the South, and warned against the "twin errors of Campbellism and Arminianism."[12]

The Abstract of Principles was intentionally modelled on the Philadelphia Confession of Faith, which was based on the Second London Confession, which in turn was a Baptist adaptation of the Westminster Confession. There was some sentiment for using the Philadelphia Confession itself as a doctrinal basis, but it was decided that a briefer statement would be better.

Where Southern Baptists differed among themselves on matters of secondary importance, the Abstract was silent. It took no stand, for example, on pre-, post-, or amillenialism, on the scope of the atonement, or the mode of inspiration. It did, however, speak clearly about the being of God, His attributes, His providence and election, salvation in Christ, the life of faith, the world to come. It was, in other words, a classic summary of what the preface to the Second London Confession called "that wholesome protestant doctrine."

Robert Lynn has said of the ideal of confessional identity that, while it has sometimes been a point of controversy, has also provided "a thread of continuity which links past, present and future."[13]

The first twenty years of the seminary's life could be called its "heroic age." Having opened its doors in 1859, it soon fell victim to the convulsions of the Civil War or, as its founders, would have put it, the War of Northern Aggression. Boyce tried unsuccessfully to gain a ministerial deferment for the students. In 1862 the seminary disbanded. Boyce and Broadus ministered as chaplains among the Confederate troops. During this time Boyce also served in the South Carolina state legislature with such distinction that he was urged on all sides to give himself entirely to political life. I have come across a poignant letter which Broadus addressed to Boyce in December of 1862:

> You have doubtless been told already that such capacities for public useful-ness ought to be permanently devoted to the public good, and all that. My dear fellow, don't listen to it. Your mission is to bring theological science into practical relation to this busy world, and if God spares your life and grants the country peace, this Seminary which was founded by your labors shall yet shine in conspicuous usefulness. Well, I have just said what I felt I must. Affectionately yours, J. A. Broadus.[14]

This same spirit prevailed on that fateful day after the war when the four founders gathered at the Boyce home in Greenville. What resources the seminary had were in useless Confederate bonds. The present looked bleak and the future bleaker. What was to be done? The four professors joined in prayer and a deep seeking of the will of God. At the end of the day Broadus said, in a line which has become famous, "Suppose we quietly agree that the Seminary may die, but we will die first."[15] All heads were silently bowed, and the matter was decided.

Boyce not only conceived and birthed the seminary but also nurtured it and kept it alive when for good reason nearly everyone expected it to die. Time and again he gave generously out of his own dwindling estate to help needy students through another semester or to pay the salaries of the other professors. In those days when there was no endowment, and no Coopera-tive Program, the seminary lived from hand to mouth, from one annual subscription campaign to the next.

In 1879 Boyce sent out a general appeal for seminary support. We do not ask for ourselves, he said ". . . but for the Seminary itself, that it may live and do its work. How much can I expect from your church or yourself between now and April 1, 1880, and how soon may we hope to receive it?" He received the following response from a certain brother, A. B. Cobb in North Carolina: "I am already contributing more than I can do with convenience to myself and comfort to my family. A salary of $6.00 a year for a pastor with seven children does not leave him much margin for contributions abroad. . . . Please don't ask me for any more." "P.S. Can't you send us a contribution to aid us in buying a new parsonage?" I don't know whether Brother Cobb was taken off the mailing list or not.

Once when the Southern Baptist Convention met in Nashville, Boyce was pleading so earnestly on behalf of the seminary that he actually burst into tears and began to weep profusely. "I would not beg for myself, or for my family like this, but for our beloved Seminary I am willing to beg." Boyce was repeatedly offered the presidency of railroads and banks and great universities, including Brown and Mercer. He declined them all to stay at Southern Seminary and fulfill his life's work, not for his own glory, nor that of the professors with whom he served, but always for the glory of God alone. *Soli deo gloria!*

Theologian and Churchman

Boyce served for thirty years as professor of systematic and polemical theology. It was one of the great regrets of his life that due to the burdens of his office he was never able to give himself fully to the discipline he loved so dearly. Yet his theology had a profound and long-lasting influence on Southern Seminary. E. Y. Mullins, whose theology of experience led to a different paradigm, nonetheless had great respect for Boyce as a theologian and continued to use his *Abstract of Systematic Theology* as a required text for the first seventeen years of his own teaching career at Southern. How are we to evaluate Boyce as theologian and churchman?

Fundamental Without Being Fundamentalist

If we accept James Barr's suggestion that fundamentalism is more a matter of attitude and perspective than of theological content, if by fundamentalist we mean narrow minded, mean spirited, obscurantist, sectarian, then Boyce was no fundamentalist. His training at Brown and Princeton, his wide reading and extensive contacts all contributed to a broad and tolerant spirit. In what I regard as his finest piece of theological reflection, Boyce wrote an extensive essay on "The Doctrine of the Suffering Christ," which was published in England in *The Baptist Quarterly* in 1870. As his apology for entering into this well-worn topic, he wrote, "It is manifestly important . . . that . . . definitions of doctrine should frequently be re-stated and re-examined. . . . It is well that they should be tested in the crucible of every age and every mind, that if there be any error it may be detected and the correction applied."[16] These are not the words of a rigid ideologue, locked in a closed system. Boyce was no fundamentalist, but he was fundamental in his adherence to the great affirmations of historic Christian orthodoxy. He was fundamental in the sense that E. Y. Mullins was fundamental when in 1923, in the midst of the evolution controversy, he addressed the Southern Baptist Convention:

We record again our unwavering adherence to the supernatural elements in the Christian religion. The Bible is God's revelation of Himself through man moved by the Holy Spirit, and is our sufficient certain and authoritative guide in religion. Jesus Christ was born of the Virgin Mary through the power of the Holy Spirit. He was the Divine and eternal Son of God. He wrought miracles, healing the sick, casting out demons, raising the dead. He died as the vicarious atoning Saviour of the world and was buried. He arose again from the dead. The tomb was emptied of its contents. In his risen body He appeared many times to His disciples. He ascended to the right hand of the Father. He will come again in person, the same Jesus who ascended from the Mount of Olives. We believe that adherence to the above truths and facts is a necessary condition of service for teachers in our Baptist schools. . . . The supreme issue today is between naturalism and supernaturalism. Teachers in our schools should be careful to free themselves from any suspicion of disloyalty on this point. . . . We pledge our support to all schools and teachers who are thus loyal to the facts of Christianity as revealed in the Scripture.[17]

Boyce, no less than Mullins, was deeply concerned about doctrine, not doctrine divorced from spiritual life, abstract and aloof, but doctrine precisely as the expression of spiritual life, dynamic and alive.

Once on a trip from the seminary, Boyce heard about certain students from Crozier Theological School who were trying to dissuade young preachers from coming to Southern because of the "antediluvian theology taught at Louisville." Boyce replied, "If my theology were not older than the days of Noah, it wouldn't be worth teaching."

On October 1, 1888, just two months before he died, Boyce wrote to Manly. With an eye to the Toy Controversy which was just beginning to subside, he said: "I greatly rejoice in the certain triumph of the truth. I feel that nothing but our own folly can prevent the success of our Seminary. If we keep things orthodox and correct within and avoid injudicious compromises while we patiently submit and laboriously labor, we shall find continuous blessing. So much do I feel this that I look back on my life's work without any apprehension of future disaster." Boyce was fundamental without being a fundamentalist.

A Reformed Baptist Without Being a Hyper-Calvinist

Boyce is famous, or infamous depending on how you look at it, for his so-called Calvinism. There is no doubt that this reputation was well deserved. One of his former students, E. E. Folk, recalled that "through the young men were generally rank Arminians when they came to the Seminary, few went through [Boyce's] course without being converted to his strong Calvinistic views."[18] Boyce had learned the doctrines of grace at the

feet of Basil Manly, Sr., and had been confirmed in them under Charles
Hodge at Princeton. But he taught these doctrines because he believed that
they were accurately and clearly set forth in Holy Scripture. As Broadus
put it, "This is believed by many of us to be really the teaching of the
Apostle Paul, as elaborated by Augustine, and systematized and defended
by Calvin."[19]

Boyce was well aware that there were some who emphasized the sovereignty of God to the exclusion of human responsibility. In the nineteenth
century a powerful hyper-Calvinist movement arose among Baptists. These
Hardshell Baptists, as they were sometimes called, opposed organized missionary work, evangelism, Sunday Schools, and especially theological seminaries which were the spawning grounds for such nefarious activities. This
led to an exclusivism which was difficult to square with the Great Commis-
sion. As one of their hymns put it.

> We are the Lord's elected few.
> Let all the rest be damned;
> There's room enough in hell for you.
> We don't want heaven crammed.

Boyce had no truck with this perspective. His zeal for the promiscuous
preaching of the gospel began in his student days and continued throughout
his life. He had a great burden for missions and organized monthly Missionary Day at the seminary which was still being held in 1960s. In 1887 when
D. L. Moody brought his evangelistic campaign to Louisville, Boyce permitted him to erect his five-thousand-seat tabernacle on seminary property
at Fifth and Broadway, while seminary professors and students served as
counselors in the inquiry room. For Boyce the sovereignty of God and the
gratuity of grace were not inhibiting but motivating factors in the witness
of the church. The doctrines of grace underscored the fact that while we
are called to be colaborers with God, all of the glory belongs to him alone.
Boyce would have agreed with what Charles H. Spurgeon, whom he greatly
admired, is alleged to have prayed: "O Lord, save all of your elect; and then
elect some more."

An Ecumenical Churchman Without Being a Denominational Relativist

In the nineteenth century the Landmark movement posed a serious threat
to Southern Seminary, a threat which culminated in the Whitsitt Controversy ten years after Boyce's death. Boyce was criticized with practicing "pulpit affiliation" with non-Baptists. Despite this criticism, both Boyce and
Broadus continued to preached regularly in non-Baptist pulpits and to

welcome non-Baptist evangelical scholars to the seminary. Ecumenical openness, a willingness to dialogue with those whom we differ, is a part of the original vision of our founders. Yet Boyce was intensely loyal to his own denomination. He served nine terms as president of the Southern Baptist Convention. In fact, he and his friend P. H. Mell of Georgia together held that office for twenty-four consecutive years. That's what you call having a corner on the market! Boyce defended Baptist distinctives such as religious liberty, separation of church and state, and believers' baptism. He resented the fact that Baptists were sometimes looked down upon by some of their co-religionists. Something of this spirit was later reflected in John R. Sampey who once found himself on a platform with representatives of more liturgical churches, who were all dressed in their clerical finery while he wore a simple suit. One of the more lavishly attired brethren looked at Sampey and asked, "To which of the sects do you belong?" Without batting an eye, Sampey replied, "To the male sex; to which of the sects do you belong?"

Boyce's theology must be seen in the context of late Protestant scholasticism, which is the intellectual milieu in which it was wrought. Boyce's theology is not infallible, as he himself would be the first to acknowledge. But in an age of relativism and secularism, which has resulted in what Thomas Altizer has called "a moment of profound theological breakdown," Boyce still stands as a model, not the only one but an important one, for the theological revitalization of the Baptist tradition. Boyce calls us back to a vision of the true and living God, not the unblinking God of a Byzantine dome, distant and aloof, but the God who meets us in mercy and judgment, the God whose favor we can never earn, but who in His sheer mercy and grace has come very close to every one of us, in a Baby in a manger, and in a Man on a cross.

The Legacy of Boyce

There are many other things I would love to tell you about Boyce: his powerful preaching, his love for little children, his concern for the poor and oppressed. He was a trustee and administrator of the Slater Fund, a major source for the endowment of black colleges during Reconstruction. All of this is a part of his legacy.

What would he say to us if he could be here today? I don't know, but I have several ideas. He would be pleased with the evidence of God's blessing on this institution. At the seminary opening in Louisville, Boyce looked into the future and envisioned the day when there would be as many as three thousand students preparing for Christian ministry in this school.

That was a bold dream in 1877. He would be pleased that his ideal of openness lives on in the Boyce Bible School, as well as in the Schools of Church Music, Christian Education, Church Social Work and Theology. He would want us to maintain the highest scholarly standards in all of our disciplines. He would be happy that we are thought of by many as the most academic seminary in the Southern Baptist Convention. He would want us to be the most academic, but he would also want us to be the godliest, the most fervent in prayer, the most missionary minded, the most evangelistically engaged, the most socially compassionate. In a time of denominational conflict and tension, I believe he would urge us, insofar as we can under God, to be ministers of reconciliation and healing. At least this is what he tried to do in his own turbulent times. He would encourage us to keep a balance between intellect and piety, openness and excellence, theology and spirituality, divine sovereignty and human responsibility from faith and free research, ecumenical witness and denominational loyalty—all of this is the legacy of Boyce. Above all, he would desire that all of our teaching and preaching and worship, our study and research, our life and witness in the world be presented as an offering to the glory of God alone.

In the summer of 1888 Boyce's health was failing when he sailed for Europe in what would be his first and last trip abroad. He died in Southern France in December 1888. Had he lived two more weeks, he would have been sixty-two years old. His body was brought back to Louisville where, on a snowy January day, he was buried in Cave Hill Cemetery. Soon thereafter an impressive monument was erected over his grave which bears this inscription: "James P. Boyce, to whom, under God, the Seminary owes its existence." Boyce's true monument, however, is not in Cave Hill Cemetery, nor in the bricks and mortar of this beautiful campus which he would have rejoiced to see. It is rather the 153 members of this faculty who over the years have affixed their signatures beneath his on the original Abstract of Principles and who have poured their lives into training men and women for the service of the church of Jesus Christ. It is scores of faithful administrators and staff members who have contributed in countless ways to the excellence of this institution. It is thousands of students who have studied here and gone out from here to serve the cause of Christ in little country churches and great urban cathedrals, in inner city chapels and far away mission fields. It is the millions of Southern Baptists who have loved this seminary and prayed for it and contributed to it. It is you and I who have somehow felt the tug of God on our lives and have come to this good place to prepare for that from which we could not turn away. All of us are the true monument of Boyce.

It is appropriate that we close this address with the words uttered at the funeral of James P. Boyce by John A. Broadus, his closest friend and fellow laborer in the founding of the seminary:

> O Brother beloved, true yokefellow through years of toil, best and dearest friend, sweet shall be thy memory till we meet again! And may there be those always ready, as the years come and go, to carry on, with widening reach and heightened power, the work we sought to do, and did begin![20]

Amen! So be it now, and God willing, so be it one hundred years from now when all of us here shall have departed from this world forever.

Notes

*This chapter is adapted from the Founder's Day address, Timothy George, delivered in the Alumni chapel of The Southern Baptist Theological Seminary on February 2, 1988.

1. James P. Boyce, "The Good Cause," *Courier-Journal,* September 3, 1877.

2. David M. Ramsey, *James Petigru Boyce: God's Gentleman* (Nashville: Sunday School Board, 1924), p. 6.

3. *Memoirs of John R. Sampey* (Nashville: Broadman press, 1947), p. 29.

4. Letter of Ellis A. Fuller to Miss Lucy Boyce, May 2, 1950. SBTS Archives.

5. John A. Broadus, *Memoir of James Petigru Boyce* (New York: A. C. Armstrong and Son, 1893), p. 54.

6. E. Brooks Holifield, *The Gentlemen Theologians* (Durham: Duke University Press, 1978), p. 218n.

7. Broadus, p. 17.

8. Ibid., p. 28.

9. *Memoirs of Sampey,* p. 30.

10. Broadus, p. 45.

11. Ibid., p. 88.

12. George, "Systematic Theology at Southern Seminary," *Review and Expositor* 82 (1985), p. 33.

13. Robert Lynn, Founder's Day, 1982.

14. Letter of Dec. 5, 1862.

15. Broadus, p. 200.

16. J. P. Boyce, "The Doctrine of the Suffering Christ," *The Baptist Quarterly* 4 (1870), p. 386.

17. *Annual of the Southern Baptist Convention, 1923,* pp. 19-20.

18. Broadus, p. 265.

19. Ibid., p. 310.

20. Ibid., p. 371.

II
Three Changes in Theological Institutions

Three Changes in Theological Institutions

(An Inaugural Address delivered before the Board of Trustees of Furman University, July 31, 1856)

I congratulate myself that I address tonight a body of men pledged to the interests of theological education and that I do it in the existence of our present relations and in the discharge of the duty assigned me. Otherwise, it might appear from the sentiments I shall utter that I am opposed to the thorough training and education of the Christian ministry. The circumstances, however, under which we have gathered together this evening indicate at once the deep interest felt by you and by myself in the cause of theological education and that, whatever sentiments may be spoken by me or heard with approbation by you, we hold the education of the ministry a matter of the first importance to the churches of Christ.

Indeed, did we think otherwise, we could no longer justly stand forth as exponents in any sense of the opinions upon this subject which prevail in our denomination. The Baptists are unmistakably the friends of education and the advocates of an educated ministry. Their twenty-four colleges and ten departments or institutions for theological instruction in this country furnish sufficient testimony to the fact that they feel the value of education and the importance, under God, of the means it affords for the better performance of the work of the ministry. And rather would I that my tongue should cleave to the roof of my mouth than that I should say anything tonight which might justly be construed into dissent from an opinion so truly in accordance with the Word of God and the enlightened sentiments of the age.

So far am I from entertaining such opinions that I would see the means of theological education increased, I would have the facilities for pursuing its studies opened to all who would embrace them, I would lead the strong men of our ministry to feel that no position is equal in responsibility or usefulness to that of one devoted to this cause, and I would spread among our churches such an earnest desire for educated ministers as would make them willing so to increase the support of the ministry as to enable those without means to anticipate the support they will receive and feel free to borrow the means by which their education may be completed.

I cannot perceive, however, how the most earnest desire for thorough theological education is inconsistent in any degree with the advocacy of the changes I propose. How can any scheme be regarded as unfavorable to that education, which, while it abates not the attainments urged upon all so far as practicable, seeks to provide such instruction as will increase the education of each individual and take the mass now uneducated and make them capable and efficient workmen for God?

The truth is that the time has come at last when the sophistry of the objection here supposed will be easily detected. The mind of the whole denomination has been awakened to the want of success under which we have suffered in our past efforts, and the best intellects and hearts in all our Southern bounds are directed in the causes of our failure and to the means by which success may be attained.

In the efforts to establish the common theological institution, proposed as a remedy for the evil, I heartily concur. I do not think that the demand for theological education calls at present for more than one institution. The experiments to be made in finally securing the best ends will be experiments for the common good and should be at the common expense. It is only by such a combination that we can procure the best and ablest instructors afforded by our denomination throughout the world. And it is, thus, only that the scheme adopted will attract sufficient notice and sympathy to test beyond doubt its value as a remedy for existing evils and as a means of developing additional changes for the improvements of theological instruction.

The recollection of past efforts to create union among us upon this subject leads many, however, to suppose that the present one will end in disappointment. I confess that many indications favor this opinion. If they be verified, and this attempt at united efforts fail, nothing will remain for us but the hope that some one of our present institutions may be able, single handed, to make the experiment for the whole and to establish the true principles of theological education.

Indeed, gentlemen, since the common institution would only have greater facilities and since the introduction of these changes, perhaps to the full extent at present necessary, will come within our power, why may we not make the experiment at once? The organization of the proposed institution will take time, especially if the location of one of our present colleges be not selected. During that time it will be incumbent upon you to provide for the instruction of the ministry. While such a time may not give opportunity for the fairest trial, especially under the circumstances of isolation in which the university stands, as the institution of a single state, yet it may be more than adequate to prove the entire practicability of the plan and to secure the honor of its inception. And more than this—should it prove successful, the knowledge of the fact will be to the denomination at large a most powerful motive for selecting this location for the common institution.

It is on this account that in performing the duty assigned me, I find myself irresistibly forced from other subjects which might have been appropriate and led to suggest to you "Three Changes in Theological Institutions," which would enable them to fulfill more adequately at least, if not completely, the hopes of their founders. These changes are intended to meet evils which, in one case by the many, in the others by the few, have been already experienced, and they are suggested as furnishing ample remedies for the existing evils.

The first evil to which I would apply a remedy is one which has been universally experienced—which, more than anything else, has shaken the faith of many in the value of theological institutions, has originated the opposition which they have at any time awakened, and has caused the mourning and sorrow of those who, having laid their foundations, still continue to cluster around them. I refer to the failure of the theological institution to call forth an abundant ministry for the churches and supply to it adequate instruction.

Whatever other purposes may have been intended to be accomplished, there can be no doubt that this has been the primary object of all our educational efforts. The university, over the interests of which you are called to preside, must for one at least be regarded as the growth of this single idea. From the very beginning of Baptist efforts for education in this state to the present moment, this has always been the mainspring of our movements. Looking back upon that band of worthies in whose minds first originated the idea of the Furman Academy and inquiring of them, and of you, gentlemen, who now hold and exercise the sacred trusts of its guardians, the objects of all the efforts put forth, I hear but one overwhelming response —that we may have an abundance of able, sound, and faithful men to proclaim the gospel of Christ, and "to feed the flocks over which the Holy Ghost shall make them overseers." The university is the offspring of prayers to the Lord of the harvest that He would send forth laborers into His harvest. It is the method our best wisdom has devised to make, through the aid of His grace, of those whom He sends in answer to our prayers, "workmen that need not to be ashamed rightly dividing the word of truth."

It is mournful that we are forced so inevitably to the conclusion that these prayers have not yet been answered and that these purposes not yet fulfilled. The theological seminary has not been a popular institution. But few have sought its advantages. But few have been nurtured by the influences sent forth from it. And while our denomination has continued to increase, and our principles have annually been spreading more widely, it has been sensibly felt that whatever ministerial increase has accompanied has been not only disproportionate to that of our membership but has owed its origin in no respect to the influence of theological education.

And this seems to be the general law in the denomination. The complaint is not peculiar to our institution. It seems to exist every where, despite all the efforts to counteract it which have been put forth; and not to be confined to Baptists, but to be the lamentation of all. You will see it in the organs of all the prominent denominations, and the cause of it is the subject of earnest inquiry.

The whitened harvest, the awakened activity of the churches, the favorable reception given to the Word of God, have never been more signally manifested. Never have been heard more piercing cries for the gospel than those with which Ethiopia accompanies her outstretched hands; never have been felt deeper longings for the coming of the kingdom of God than are uttered by praying hearts throughout Christendom; never has sin appeared to develop more fearful evils; never has "hydra headed error" so fully or so variously exalted herself; neither has God ever multiplied to so gracious an extent the means which He gives the church as an aid to the ministry not to diminish its labors, but to make them fourfold more abundant and an hundred-fold more valuable. The world seems ready, lying at the very door of the Christian church, yet calling for laborious efforts to gather it in. Oh! were there ever a time when we would expect that God would answer the prayers of His churches and overflood the land and the world with a ministry adequate to uphold His cause in every locality, it should seem to be now—now, when the wealth of the churches is sufficient to send the gospel to every creature, now, when, in the art of printing, the church has again received the gift of tongues; now, when the workings of God Himself indicate His readiness to beget a nation in a day; now, when the multiplication a thousand fold of the labourers will still leave an abundant work for each; but now, alas! now, when our churches at home are not adequately supplied; when dark and destitute places are found in the most favored portions of our own land; when the heathen are at our very doors,

and the cry is help, and there is no help because there are not laborers
enough to meet the wants immediately around us.

There are serious questions presented to us here. To what are these things
due? Have we not disregarded the laws which the providence and Word of
God have laid down for us? And does He not now chastise us by suffering
our schemes to work out their natural results, that we, being left to ourselves, may see our folly and return to Him and to His ways as the only
means of strength!

In ascribing this evil for the most part to our theological institutions, I
would not appear unmindful of other circumstances upon which an increase
of the ministry in our churches depends. Never would I consent to lift my
voice upon such a subject as this without a distinct recognition of the
sovereignty of God working His own will and calling forth, according to
that will, that many or the few with whose aid He will secure the blessing.
Never could I proceed upon any assumption that would seem to take for
granted that there is not the utmost need of more special awakening to
devotion and piety in our churches and a more fervent utterance of prayer
for the increase of the laborers. Neither would I have it supposed that all
that the theological institution can effect will be fully adequate to our wants
while our pastors neglect to search out and encourage the useful gifts which
God has bestowed upon the members of their churches or the churches
themselves neglect the law of God which provides an adequate support for
the ministry. But while due prominence is given to all of these circumstances, it yet appears that the chief cause is to be found in our departure
from the way which God has marked out for us and our failure to make
provision for the education of such a ministry as He designs to send forth
and honor.

Permit me to ask what has been the prominent idea at the basis of
theological education in this country? To arrive at it we have only to notice
the requisitions necessary for entrance upon a course of study. Have they
not been almost universally that the student should have passed through a
regular college course or made attainments equivalent thereto? And have
not even the exceptional cases been rare instances in which the faculty or
board have, under peculiar circumstances, assumed the responsibility of a
deviation from the ordinary course?

The idea, which is prominent as the basis of this action, is that the work
of the ministry should be entrusted only to those who have been classically
educated—an assumption which singularly enough is made for no other
profession. It is in vain to say that such is not the theory or the practice
of our denomination. It is the theory and the practice of by far the larger

portion of those who have controlled our institutions and have succeeded in engrafting this idea upon them, contrary to the spirit which prevails among the churches. They have done this without doubt in the exercise of their best judgment, but have failed because they neglected the better plan pointed out by the providence and Word of God.

The practical operation of this theory has tended in two ways to diminish the ranks of our valuable ministry. It has restrained many from entering upon the work and has prevented the arrangement of such a course of study as would have enabled those who have entered upon it to fit themselves in a short time for valuable service. The consequences have been that the number of those who have felt themselves called of God to the ministry has been disproportioned to the wants of the churches; and of that number but a very small proportion have entered it with a proper preparation for even common usefulness. And only by energy and zeal, awakened by their devotion to the work, have they been able to succeed in their labors, and to do for themselves the work, the greater part of which the theological school should have accomplished for them.

In His Word and in His providence, God seems to have plainly indicated the principle upon which the instruction of the ministry should be based. It is not that every man should be made a scholar, an adept in philology, an able interpreter of the Bible in its original languages, acquainted with all the sciences upon the various facts and theories of which God's Word is attacked and must be defended, and versed in all the systems of true and false philosophy. Indeed, some must understand these in order to encounter the enemies which attack the very foundations of religion. But while the privilege of becoming such shall be freely offered to all, and every student shall be encouraged to obtain all the advantages that education can afford, the opportunity should be given to those who cannot or will not make thorough scholastic preparation to obtain that adequate knowledge of the truths of the Scriptures systematically arranged and of the laws which govern the interpretation of the text in the English version, which constitutes all that is actually necessary to enable them to preach the gospel, to build up the churches on their most holy faith, and to instruct them in the practice of the duties incumbent upon them.

The scriptural qualifications of the ministry do, indeed, involve the idea of knowledge, but that knowledge is not of the sciences nor of philosophy nor of the languages, but of God and of His plan of salvation. He who has not this knowledge, though he be learned in all the learning of the schools, is incapable of preaching the Word of God. But he who knows it, not superficially, not merely in those plain and simple declarations known to every believing reader, but in the power, as revealed in its precious and sanctifying doctrines, is fitted to bring forth out of his treasury things new and old, and is a workman that needeth not to be ashamed, although he may speak to his hearers in uncouth words or in manifest ignorance of all the sciences. The one belongs to the class of educated ministers, the other to the ministry of educated men, and the two things are essentially different.

The one may be a Bunyan, unlearned withal, and in many respects ignorant, rough and rugged of speech, with none of the graces of the orator or the refinement of the rhetorician, but so filled with the grace abounding to the chief of sinners, so learned in the Scriptures quoted at every point for the support of the truth he speaks, and discoursing such sweet and godly doctrine, that he is manifest as one taught so truly in the gospel that the most learned scholars may sit silently at his feet and learn the wonders of the Word of God. The other may be a Parker, with all the grace and polish of the finished scholar, pouring forth the purest and most powerful English, able to illustrate and defend his cause by contributions from every store-house of knowledge, presenting attractions in his oratory which induce his educated audience to receive or to overlook his blasphemous doctrines, yet so destitute of the knowledge of true Christianity and of a genuine experience of the influences of the Holy Ghost, that he denies the plainest doctrines of the Bible, saps the very foundation of all revealed truth, and manifests so profound an ignorance of the Book he undertakes to expound and the religion of which he calls himself a Minister that the humblest Christian among our very servants shall rise up in condemnation against him in the great day of accounts.

Who is the minister here—the man of the schools or the man of the Scriptures? Who bears the insignia of an ambassador for Christ? Whom does God own? Whom would the church hear? In whose power would she put forth her strength? And yet these instances, though extreme, will serve to show what may be the ministry of the educated man and what that of the illiterate man, the educated minister. The perfection of the ministry, it is gladly admitted, would consist in the just combination of the two; but it is not the business of the church to establish a perfect, but an adequate ministry—and it is only of the latter that we may hope for an abundant supply. The qualification God lays down is the only one He permits us to demand, and the instruction of our theological schools must be based upon such a plan as shall afford this amount of education to those who actually constitute the mass of our ministry and who cannot obtain more.

The providential dispensation of God, in the administration of the affairs of His church, fully illustrate the truth of this principle, so plainly in accordance with His Word. That the education of the schools is of great advantage to the minister truly trained in the word of truth has been illustrated by the labors of Paul, Augustine, Calvin, Beza, Davies, Edwards, and a host of others who have stood forth in their different ages the most prominent of all the ministry of their day and the most efficient workmen in the cause of Christ. While in the eleven apostles, in the mass of the ministry of that day, and of all other times and places, God has manifested that He will work out the greater proportion of His purposes by men of no previous training and educated only in the mysteries of that truth which is in Christ Jesus.

Never has He illustrated that principle more fully than in connection with the progress of the principles of our own denomination. We have had our men of might and power who have shown the advantages of scholastic education as a basis, but we have also seen the great instruments of our progress to have been the labors of a much humbler class. Trace our history back, either through the centuries that have long passed away or in the workings of God during the last hundred years, and it will be seen that the mass of the vineyard laborers have been from the ranks of fishermen and tax gatherers, cobblers and tinkers, weavers and ploughmen, to whom God has not disdained to impart gifts, and whom He has qualified as His ambassadors by the presence of that Spirit by which, and not by might, wisdom or power, is the work of the Lord accomplished.

The Baptists of America, especially, should be the last to forget this method of working on the part of their Master and the first to retrace any steps which would seem to indicate such forgetfulness. It has been signally manifested in the establishment of their faith and principles. The names which have been identified with our growth have been those of men of no collegiate education, of no learning or rhetorical eloquence, of no instruction even in schools of theology. Hervey, Gano, Bennet, Semple, Broadus, Armstrong, Mercer, who were these? Men of education, of collegiate training, of theological schools? Nay, indeed. All praise to those who did possess any of these advantages. They were burning and shining lights. They hid neither talents nor opportunities, but devoted them to the cause they loved, and accomplished much in its behalf. They maintained positions which perhaps none others could have occupied. But their number was not sufficient for the work of the Lord, and He gave a multitude of others—men who were found in labors oft, in wearisome toils by day and by night, in heat or in cold, facing dangers of every kind, enduring private and public persecution, travelling through swamp and forest to carry the glad tidings of salvation to the lost and perishing of our country. And the Baptists can neither forget them nor the principle taught us in their labors, by the providence of God. Whatever may be the course of those who have the training of their ministry, these ideas have sunk so deeply into the minds of the denomination that they can never be eradicated. And the day will yet come, perhaps has already come, when the churches will rise in their strength and demand that our theological institutions make educational provisions for the mass of their ministry.

I have spoken of our ministry in the past as composed of men whose success illustrates the theory of the need only of theological education. And yet it is apparent that they enjoyed none of the advantages for that purpose which are connected with the present arrangements for study. In the absence of these, however, they did attain to the amount of theological education which is essential. This was accomplished through excessive labor exercised by minds, capable of mighty efforts, and drawn forth under circumstances favorable to their development.

When we look attentively at the record they have left us, or contemplate those of them whom God's mercy to us permits yet to linger with us, we perceive that they were not the uneducated ministers commonly supposed. It is true, as has been said, that they had not the learning of the schools. A few books of theology—perhaps a single commentary—formed, with their Bibles, their whole apparatus of instruction and measured the extent of their reading. But of these books they were wont to make themselves masters. By a course of incessant study, accompanied by examinations of the Word of God, they were so thoroughly imbued with the processes and results of the best thoughts of their authors that they became, for all practicable purposes, almost the same men. And if, by any course of training, substantially of the same kind, our theological schools can restore to us such a mass ministry as was then enjoyed, the days of our progress and prosperity will be realized to have but just begun. And we shall go forward, by the help of the Lord, to possess the whole land which lieth before us. If by any means to these can be added at least five-fold the number of those now educated in the regular course of theology, I doubt not but it will be felt that the most sanguine hopes they have ever excited will be more than fulfilled.

I believe, gentlemen, that it can be done; and more than this, that in the attempt to do it, we shall accomplish an abundantly greater work. Let us abandon the false principle which has so long controlled us and adopt the one which God points out to us by His Word and His providence and from the very supplies God now gives to us may be wrought out precisely such a ministry. Those who have entered upon the work will be rendered fully capable to perform its duties, and numbers besides will be called forth to it who have heretofore been restrained by insurmountable obstacles.

Let such a change be made in the theological department as shall provide an English course of study for those who have only been able to attain a plain English education. Let that course comprise the evidences of Christianity, systematic and polemic theology, the rules of interpretation applied to the English version; some knowledge of the principles of rhetoric, extensive practice in the development from texts of subjects and skeletons of sermons, whatever amount of composition may be expedient, and full instruction in the nature of pastoral duties—let the studies of this course be so pursued as to train the mind to habits of reflection and analysis, to awaken it to conceptions of the truths of Scripture, to fill it with arguments from the Word of God in support of its doctrines, and to give it facility in constructing and presenting such arguments—and the work will be accomplished.

Experience alone can determine the length of time such a course should occupy. It should be so arranged for two years, however, that the better prepared and the more diligent may be able to pass over it in one. Doubtless this would be done by the vast majority, at least of those of riper years.

By the means proposed, the theological school will meet the wants of a large class of those who now enter the ministry without the advantages of such instruction—a class equally with their more learned associates burning with earnest zeal for the glory of God and deep convictions of the value of immortal souls, one possessed of natural gifts, capable even with limited knowledge of enchaining the attention, affecting the hearts and enlightening the minds of many who surround them. A class composed, however, of those who, with few exceptions, soon find themselves exhausted of their materials, forced to repeat the same topics in the same way, and finally to aim at nothing but continuous exhortation, bearing constantly upon the same point, or as is oftentimes the case, destitute of any point at all. In their present condition, these ministers are of comparatively little value to the churches, having no capacity to feed them with the Word of God, affording no attractions to bring a congregation to the house of God, and no power to set before them such an exposition of the Word of God as may, through the influences of His Spirit, awaken them to penitence and lead to faith in the Lord Jesus Christ. What the same men might become were they better instructed is apparent from the results attained by men of the same previous education, who, possessed of more leisure or of a greater natural taste for study, have so improved themselves as to occupy positions of greater respectability and usefulness.

The class of men whose cause I now plead before you is of all those which furnish material for our ministry, that which most needs the theological training I would ask for it. Every argument for theological schools bears directly in favor of its interests. Are such schools founded that our ministry may not be ignorant of the truth? Which class of that ministry is more ignorant than this? Is the object of their endowment that such education may be cheapened? Who are generally in more straitened circumstances? Is it designed to produce an abundant, able, faithful and practical ministry? Where are the materials more abundant? Whence, for the amount of labor expended, will come more copious harvests? So that it appears that whatever may be our obligations to other classes, or the advantages to be gained in their education, the mere statement of them impresses upon us our duty and the yet greater advantages to be gained by the education of that class which should comprise two-thirds at least of those who receive a theological education.

The men who go from college walls untaught in theology have yet a training and an amount of knowledge of incalculable benefit. They can do something to make up their deficiencies. But what chance is there for these others? They know not how to begin to study. Let one of them take up the Scriptures, and he finds himself embarrassed in the midst of statements which the church, for centuries after the apostles, had not fully harmonized —statements which constitute the facts of theology, from which, in like manner with other sciences, by processes of induction and comparison, the absolute truth must be established. If, to escape the difficulty, he turns to a textbook of theology, he is puzzled at once by technicalities so easily understood by those better instructed, that this technical character is totally unperceived. If he turns in this dilemma to our seminaries, he finds no encouragement to enter.

A man of age, perhaps of family, he is called upon to spend years of study in the literary and scientific departments before he is allowed to suppose that he can profitably pursue theology. Straitened, perhaps, in his circumstances and unwilling to partake of the bounty of others, he is told that he must study during a number of years, during which his expenses would probably exhaust five-fold his little store. With a mind capable of understanding and perceiving the truth, and of expressing judicious opinions upon any subject, the facts of which he comprehends, he is told that he must pass through a course of study, the chief value of which is to train the mind, and which will only benefit him by the amount of knowledge it will incidentally convey. I can readily imagine the despair with which that man would be filled who, impelled by a conviction that it is his duty to preach the gospel, contemplates under these circumstances the provisions which the friends of an educated ministry have made for him. We know not how many affected by that sentiment are at this moment longing to enter upon preparation for a work which they feel God has entrusted only to those who, because of their knowledge of His Word, have an essential element of aptness to teach. Be it yours, gentlemen, to reanimate their drooping hopes by opening up before them the means of attaining this qualification.

The adoption of the true principle will not only tend, however, to secure for us this education in the masses, which we need, but will also increase five-fold the number of those who will receive a thorough theological education. It will do this by the change of policy to which it will lead in reference to another class of our candidates for the ministry.

We have among us a number of men who have enjoyed all the advantages of college life, but who have not been able, or willing, to spend the additional years needed for theological study. These are possessed of far greater advantages than those of the other class, men of polished education, of well trained minds, capable of extensive usefulness to the cause of Christ, but their deficiencies are plainly apparent and readily traceable to the lack of a theological education. They are educated men, but not educated ministers, for, while familiar with all the sciences which form parts of the college curriculum, they are ignorant for the most part of that very science which lies at the foundation of all their ministerial labors. The labors of their pastoral charges prevent such study of the Word of God, either exegetically or systematically, as will enable them to become masters of its contents. Having entered upon the work of the ministry, however, they are forced to press forward, encountering difficulties at every step—fearing to touch upon many doctrines of Scripture, lest they misstate them—and frequently guilty of such misstatements, even in the presentation of the simpler topics they attempt, because they fail to recognize the important connections which exist among all the truths of God.

A few, indeed, possessed of giant minds capable of the most accurate investigation and filled with indomitable energy in the pursuit of what they feel to be needful, overcome every obstacle and attain to knowledge often superior to that of others whose training has been more advantageous. But the vast majority find themselves burdened with a weight which they cannot remove and by which they feel that their energies are almost destroyed.

It is needless to say of these that the churches do not grow under their ministry; that, not having partaken of strong meat, they cannot impart it. Their hearers pass on from Sabbath to Sabbath, awakened, indeed, to practical duties, made in may respects efficient in cooperating with Christ's people, but not built up to this condition on their most holy faith, but upon other motives which, however good, are really insufficient for the best progress, at least of their own spiritual natures. Such is not the position of the ministry which four-fifths of our educated men should occupy. They will tell you themselves, gentlemen, that this should not be the case. If due to their own precipitancy, they will attach blame to themselves, but if it result from the exclusiveness of theological schools, their declaration is equivalent to testimony in favor of its removal, and of the admission of all who are capable of pursuing the regular course to participate in its advantages. The disturbances felt about unsettled doctrines, the inability experienced to declare the whole counsel of God, the doctrinal mistakes realized as frequently committed, have long since convinced them that all of their other education is of but little value compared with that knowledge of theology which they have lost in its acquisition.

The theory of the theological school should doubtless be to urge upon every one to take full courses in both departments; but when this is not possible, it should give to those who are forced to select between them the opportunity of omitting the collegiate and entering at once upon the theological course. I see not how any one can rationally question that many, if not all of those who are fitted for the sophomore, or even the freshman class in college, are prepared, so far as knowledge of books or languages is concerned, to enter with very great, though not with the utmost profit, upon the study of theology. The amount of Greek and Latin acquired, is ample for this purpose. The study of Hebrew and Chaldee are commenced in the theological course, while that which is really the main object for the younger men in the collegiate course, the training and forming of the mind so far as at all practicable, will for the older students have been already accomplished, or for them and for the younger ones may be compensated in great part by the more thorough training in the studies of the seminary, necessary to all who would acquire such knowledge of theology as will make them fully acquainted with its truths.

Since this is the case, why compel this class to spend their time in studies which, however valuable in themselves, have but a secondary importance, compared with those they are made to supersede? If there be any who will pursue the studies of both departments, their number will never be diminished by the adoption of the plan proposed. If it will, better that this be so than that so many others neglect theology. But we may confidently believe that the results will only be to take from the collegiate course those who would neglect the other and cause them to spend the same number of years in the study of that which has an immediate bearing upon their work. It is simply a choice as to certain men between a thorough literary and a thorough theological course. The former may make a man more refined and intelligent, better able to sustain a position of influence with the world, and more capable of illustrating, by a wide range of science, the truth he may have arrived at. The latter will improve his Christian graces, will impart to him the whole range of revealed truth, will make him the instructor of His people, truly the man of God prepared in all things to give to each one his portion in due season.

The bare announcement of the changes proposed in the application of our principle will show that but little additional provision will be needed to put it into operation. The same course of systematic theology will be sufficient for all classes—the advantages possessed by those more highly educated, enabling them simply to add to the text-book or lectures, the examination of Turretine, or some other prescribed author. In the study of Scripture interpretation, it may be necessary to make two divisions, though experience will probably prove the practicability even of uniting these. There will be needed for all classes the same instruction in the evidences of Christianity, the pastoral theology, in the analysis of texts, the construction of skeletons, and the composition of essays and sermons; and in all of these the classes may be united. So that, really, we will only so far revolutionize the institution, as to add numbers to the classes, and permit some of those who we add, to take up those studies only which the plain English education will enable them to pursue profitably. All the inconvenience which may accrue therefrom will be gladly endured by all for the benefit of the masses, and because of the mutual love and esteem which, by their throwing together, will be fostered between the most highly educated and the plainest of our ministry.

Is it too much, gentlemen, to ask that this experiment may be tried? Does it not seem practicable? Are not the fruits it would produce, if brought to a successful issue, an ample inducement to us to venture upon an experiment so likely to succeed, and which, if unsuccessful, can so easily be abandoned? And would not that trial seem to put the institution upon the basis of that principle which God has established, and which we may therefore expect him to bless by sending forth, as the Lord of the harvest, an abundance of laborers into the harvest?

In adopting this change, we are so far from saying that education is unnecessary that we proclaim its absolute necessity. We undertake, however, to point out what education it is that is, thus, essential and we provide the means by which adequate theological instruction may be given to the four-fifths of our ministry who now enjoy no means of instruction. We look with confidence for the blessing of God upon this plan, not because we believe that He favors an ignorant ministry, but because we know that He requires that His ministry be instructed, and by His Word and His providence He has pointed out the nature of the learning He demands. We believe that the plan proposed is based upon these indications; and that His refusal to send forth laborers has been chastisement inflicted upon us that we may be brought back to His own plans, which we have abandoned for those of men.

I proceed now to speak more briefly of a second change needed in our theological institutions, by which it is to be hoped they will be enabled to produce scholars adequate to the exigencies of our own denomination and to the common cause of Christianity. It is singularly enough the case that, while they have abandoned the education of the masses for the thorough training of the few, God has not permitted them to accomplish the very object made most prominent in their pretensions. It is not to be concealed that upon this point a dissatisfaction exists which, though not so general, has taken deep root in the minds of our better educated laymen and ministers.

I refer not now to the charge that there has been want of practical training by which those who have taken a theological course. This evil, which I believe may be justly urged against the instruction of every theological institution in our country, is to be attributed to the fact that the professors place the means of instruction in the hands of their students without exercising over their pursuit of those studies the superintendence which is needed. The remedy for this evil is the adoption of that method of instruction which should have marked the previous collegiate course. The studies should be so pursued as to call forth and improve all the powers of analysis and synthesis in the consideration of the subjects presented. Then the student must have practice in the quick production of his thoughts, as well as in deriving the appropriate subject from his text, and in forming skeletons of discourses. Thus, he will not only be fully acquainted with the truth but also able to present it readily and appropriately upon all occasions. If this course be pursued, and the student be encouraged at the same time to engage in every practical work, such as instructing in Sabbath Schools and Bible classes, conducting social meetings in destitute places, preaching where the only ambition will be to present the truth plainly and simply, the complaints about the lack of efficient and practical training in theological students will not longer be heard.

Neither do I allude to the inability of our institutions to compel the attendance of those immediately about them who seek the highest attainments. To remove this, the department must also secure a sufficient number of ablest men, the course must be extended to three years, so as to furnish time for the pursuit of the widest range of study, and the practical training already referred to being then adopted, the superior advantages afforded would soon manifest themselves in the character of the scholarship and the ministry it would send forth. Under such training, the same material would be made doubly as efficient as under that of any of our present institutions.

The dissatisfaction to which I refer, has been awakened by the inadequate extent to which all theological institutions have pursued their studies, and the consequent lack among us of the scholarship which prevails in some countries abroad. It has been felt as a sore evil, that we have been dependent in great part upon the criticism of Germany for all the more learned investigations in biblical criticism and exegesis, and that in the study of the development of the doctrine of the church, as well as of its outward progress, we have been compelled to depend upon works in which much of error has been mingled with truth, owing to the defective standpoint occupied by their authors.

And although the disadvantages of American scholars have been realized as arising from the want of adequate theological libraries, as well as from the inaccessible nature of much other material, it has been felt that it has also been in great part due to the limited extent to which the study of theological science has been pursued among us. We have been much dependent upon others and unable to push forward investigations for ourselves and even so inadequately acquainted with the valuable results of others who have accomplished the work for us. Only a few perhaps have participated in this sentiment, but the evil which awakens it is not, therefore, the less momentous.

It is an evil which may be regarded as pervading the whole field of American religious scholarship, and the remedy should be sought alike by all denominations. It is a matter of the deepest interest to all, that we should be placed in a position of independence in this matter, and that our rising ministry should be trained under the scholarship of the Anglo Saxon mind, which, from its nature, as well as from the circumstances which surround it, is eminently fitted to weigh evidence and to decide as to its appropriateness and its proper limitations. But the obligation resting on the Baptist denomination is far higher than this. It extends not merely to matters of detail, but to those of vital interest. The history of religious literature, and of Christian scholarship, has been a history of Baptist wrongs. We have been overlooked, ridiculed and defamed. Critics have committed the grossest perversions, violated the plainest rules of criticism, and omitted points which could not have been developed without benefit to us. Historians who have professed to write the history of the church, have either utterly ignored the presence of those of our faith or classed them among fanatics and heretics or, if forced to acknowledge the prevalence of our principles and practice among the earliest churches, have adopted such false theories as to church power, and the development and growth of the truth and principles of Scripture, that by all, save their most discerning readers, our pretensions to an early origin and a continuous existence, have been rejected.

The Baptists in the past have been entirely too indifferent to the position they, thus, occupy. The have depended too much upon the known strength of their principles and the ease with which from Scripture they could defend them. They have, therefore, neglected many of those means which extensive learning affords and which have been used to great advantage in support of other opinions. It is needless to say, gentlemen, that we can no longer consent to occupy this position. We owe a change to ourselves—as Christians, bound to show an adequate reason for the differences between us and others—as men of even moderate scholarship, that it may appear that we have not made the gross errors in philology and criticism, which we must have made if we be not right—as the successors of a glorious spiritual ancestry illustrated by heroic martyrdom, by the profession of noble principles, buy the maintenance of true doctrine—as the Church of Christ, which He has ever preserved as the witness of His truth, by which He has illustrated His wonderful ways, and shown that His promises are sure and steadfast. Nay, we owe it to Christ Himself, whose truth we hold so distinctively as to separate us from all others of His believing people.

But the question arises, how can we avoid it? The amplest course now afforded, gives to students but slight preparation for entrance upon such duties. Our ministry receives no such support as warrants the purchase of more than moderate libraries. The labors of most of our pastoral charges are sufficient fully to occupy the time of those upon whom they are devoted. And how shall we avoid it?

It is a ray of hope to us, gentlemen, that even under these disadvantageous circumstances, some are taking steps to this end. There are men of such indomitable energy, so fertile of resources and so full of faith, that no work seems too great to undertake and no difficulties too serious to overcome. And some of these are already among us, and justice shall not altogether be long refused us. But the men of whom I speak are too rare, and the obligation which we owe, too great for us to be thus content. We must provide facilities to these and necessities to others if we would yet occupy our true position.

It is scarcely necessary to remark that any plan which can be devised must be based upon the presence in the institution of a good theological library—one which shall not only be filled with the gathered lore of the past but also endowed with the means of annual increase. Without this, no institution can pursue extensive courses of study or contribute anything directly to the advancement of learning. The professor is cut off from valuable and necessary books and the student hindered from making even the least important investigations in the course of study he is pursuing.

The plan I propose to you supposes the possession of such a library; and this, even if it be such, is its only peculiar item of expense. It has occurred to me that an additional course of study might be provided for those who may be graduates of theological institutions. This course might extend over one or two years, according to the amount of study the student may propose to accomplish. In it the study of the Oriental languages might be extended to the Arabic and the Syriac. The writing of exegetical thesis would furnish subjects for investigation and give a more ample acquaintance with the original text and with the laws of its interpretation. The textbooks or lectures studied in systematic and polemic theology could be compared with kindred books, the theories of opponents examined in their own writings, and notes taken for future use from rare and costly books. These and similar studies which should be laid down in a well-digested course would bestow accurate scholarship, train the student in the methods of original investigation, give him confidence in the results previously attained, and open to him resources from which he might draw extensively in interpreting the Scriptures and in setting forth the truths they contain. The result would be that a band of scholars would go forth from almost every one of whom we might expect valuable contributions to our theological literature.

It is to be expected that but few would take advantage of this course. Such would certainly be the case at first. The only result would be that but little additional provision will be needed. Two additional recitations a week for each of three or four professors would be more than adequate. And though such students should not be more than a twentieth part of those graduated, though not more than one each year, will not their value to the denomination more than counterbalance the little additional attention which will, thus, be given?

Were the production of this kind of scholars the only advantage to be gained, we might readily rest upon this the advocacy of this change. But there are others connected with it which may still further commend it by an apparently more practical tendency. I have mentioned the Arabic as one of its studies. The knowledge of that language would be of obvious value to those who go forth as missionaries to Central Africa. Mohammedanism is there the only form of religion, which is violently opposed to the truth, and the language of the Koran is a medium of common intercourse. This, however, would be but trifling, as compared with those common to all our missionaries, who may be instructed in such a course. The results of past missionary efforts, appear to indicate that we, like the apostles, must adopt the system of home laborers, if we would evangelize the world. We must get natives to proclaim the glad tidings of salvation. The men whom we send forth to missionary stations must then be qualified to instruct the native preachers in all the elements of theological education. They will not only have to put the Bible into their hands as a textbook, but they will have to prepare, in the native language, or translate into it such books of theology, as shall give them adequate instruction. There are but few of those who take the ordinary course that are capable of this. Theology is not a science so easily understood, and a mistake about which is of such slight importance, that the instructor in it dares attempt his work without ample investigation. In the course of missionary labors, many years must, therefore, elapse before opportunity can be gained for such research; and if this be afforded, the missionary, with his few books, limited time, and weighty responsibilities, will still feel the great importance of the advantages gained from this course and will be grateful to that institution which has placed it within his reach. And while from this class we would furnish such instruction abroad, would it not be to them also that our institutions at home would chiefly look for their professors? And though there were no others to take advantage of its additional instruction, would not the impetus given to these, the love of learning which would be begotten, the ready preparation to enter at once upon any field to which they might be called, and the number from which we might select the most competent, be ample inducements to lay down this additional course?

I have striven, gentlemen, merely to suggest the benefits to be derived. Multiply and develop them for yourselves, and realize the results. I cannot see how any conception can arise which will prove extravagant. Learning will abound among us. The world will be subdued to Christ. The principles dear to our hearts will universally prevail.

The change which I would in the last place propose is not intended to meet an evil existing in our theological institutions so much as one which is found in the denomination at large, and which may at some future time injuriously affect this educational interest. It is the adoption of a declaration of doctrine to be required of those who assume the various professorships.

The most superficial observer must perceive that in our day the sound doctrine of our churches is much imperiled. Campbellism, though checked in every direction in which it attempted to develop itself, has left no little of its leaven among us and exerts no inconsiderable influence. The distinctive principles of Arminianism have also been engrafted upon many of our churches; and even some of our ministry have not hesitated publicly to avow them. That sentiment, the invariable precursor, or accompaniment of all heresy—that the doctrines of theology are matters of mere speculation, and its distinctions only logomachines and technicalities, has obtained at least a limited prevalence. And the doctrinal sentiments of a large portion of the ministry and membership of the churches are seen to be either very much unsettled or radically wrong.

Sad will be the day for this university should such sentiments ever obtain prevalence in your board or receive the sanction of any of your theological professors. And yet that this is not impossible is evident from the history of others similarly situated. The day has already come when it has been made matter of congratulation in a Baptist journal of high standing that at the examination of perhaps the best endowed and most flourishing Baptist theological seminary in America the technical terms of theology were no longer heard.

A crisis in Baptist doctrine is evidently approaching, and those of us who still cling to the doctrines which formerly distinguished us have the important duty to perform of earnestly contending for the faith once delivered to the saints. Gentlemen, God will call us to judgment if we neglect it.

The evil is one which calls for the adoption of a remedy by every church and every minister among us. It demands that every doctrine of Scripture be determined and expressed and that all should see to it; the churches which call and the Presbyteries which ordain, that those set apart to preach the word be men "whose faith the Churches may follow," "who take heed to themselves and the doctrine," and "are not as many who corrupt the word of God."*

[*It is not my design here to urge that the same abstract of faith be applied in like manner to members of churches, to ministers and to theological professors. It is right that the doctrine held by every church should be distinctly declared but Scripture and experience teach that many members are as yet babes in Christ and, therefore, not prepared to express that knowledge of the doctrine of the word to be expected of those who are teachers thereof. The apostolic rule in such cases is plain—"him that is weak in the faith receive ye, but not to doubtful disputations" (Rom. 14:1). If, therefore, an applicant for membership gives evidence of a change of heart and is so far convinced of the truth of these peculiarities which mark us as a denomination as to desire to unite with us, he should be admitted—it being admitted that he is not to disturb the church about any different opinion he may entertain until by thorough examination of the Scriptures he has satisfied himself that the church is in error.

While, however, this is all that should be required of a member of the church, we should ask of one of its ministers such an agreement to its expressed doctrine as should be even more than substantial. The points of difference here allowable are very trivial, being such as will not in any respect interfere in his ministrations with that fullness of agreement of Scripture truth, through which he is enabled to preach the word of God without danger of misleading his people in any particular.

But of him who is to teach the ministry, who is to be the medium through which the fountain of Scripture truth is to flow to them—whose opinions more than those of any living man, are to mold their conceptions of the doctrines of the Bible, it is manifest that much more is requisite. No difference, however slight, no peculiar sentiments, however speculative, is here allowable. His agreement with the standard should be exact. His declaration of it should be based upon no mental reservation, upon no private understanding with those who immediately invest him into office; but the articles to be taught having been fully and distinctly laid down, he should be able to say from his knowledge of the Word of God that he knows these articles to be an exact summary of the truth therein contained. If the summary of truth established be incorrect, it is the duty of the board to change it, if such change be within their power; if not, let an appeal be made to those who have the power, and if there be none such, then far better is it that the whole endowment be thrown aside than that the principle be adopted that the professor sign any abstract of doctrine with which he does not agree and in accordance with which he does not intend to teach. No professor should be allowed to enter upon such duties as are there undertaken, with the understanding that he is at liberty to modify the truth, which he has been placed there to inculcate.

I have added this note that my meaning upon this point may not be misconceived. The same principle of Scripture lies at the foundation of the requirements here proposed for members of churches, ministers and theological professors; and it is to that principle that I refer above. But its application is confined to the necessity of the case. In the church the great essential to membership is that a genuine work of grace be evidenced. Hence we apply a test sufficient to secure this. In the ministry, it is essential, however, that the Word of God be preached in its purity and power. Hence must a minister be not only a converted man, but one acquainted even more than substantially with the system of truth taught in the Bible. But the theological professor is to teach ministers, to place the truth, and all the errors connected with it in such a manner before his pupils, that they shall arrive at the truth without danger of any mixture of error therewith. He cannot do this if he have any erroneous tendencies, and hence his opinions must be expressly affirmed to be upon every point in accordance with the truth we believe to be taught in the Scriptures. What is here laid down as the application of the principle referred to above, is essential respectively in each of the relations sustained to us, to give us that confidence in the individual which will secure to him our Christian sympathy, support and fellowship.]

Peculiar obligations rest, however, upon those to whom are entrusted the education of the rising ministry. God in His mercy preserve the instructors from the crime of teaching a single error, however unimportant, and grant unto all our boards the grace necessary for faithfulness to the trusts developed upon them, that false doctrine, however trifling, may receive no countenance.

It is with a single man that error usually commences; when such a man has influence or position, it is impossible to estimate the evil that will attend it. Ecclesiastical history is full of warning upon this subject. Scarcely a single heresy has ever blighted the church which has not owed its existence, or its development, to that one man of power and ability whose name has always been associated with its doctrines. And yet seldom has an opinion been thus advanced, which has not subsequently had its advocate in every age, and which is some ages has not extensively prevailed.

The history of our own denomination in this country furnishes an illustration. Playing upon the prejudices of the weak and ignorant among our people, decrying creeds as an infringement upon the rights of conscience, making a deep impression by his extensive learning and great abilities, Alexander Campbell threatened at one time the total destruction of our faith. Had he occupied a chair in one of our theological institutions, that destruction might have been completed. There would have been time to disseminate widely and fix deeply his principles before it became necessary to avow them publicly; and when this necessity arrived, it would have been attended by the support of the vast majority of our best educated ministers. Who can estimate the evil which would then have ensued!

The danger which threatened in this instance may assail us again. Another such, and yet another, may arise and, favored by better circumstances, may instill false principles into the minds of his pupils, and sending them forth to occupy the prominent pulpits of the land, may influence all our churches, and the fair fabric of our faith may be entirely demolished.

This it is that should make us tremble when we think of our theological institutions. If there be any instrument of our denominational prosperity which we should guard at every point, it is this. The doctrinal sentiments of the faculty are of far greater importance than the proper investment and expenditure of its funds, and the trusts devolved upon those who watch over its interests should in that respect, if in any, be sacredly guarded.

For all the purposes aimed at, no other test can be equally effective with that confession of faith acknowledged in the Charleston Baptist Association —the doctrines of which had almost universal prevalence in this state at the time of the foundation of the institution. Let that then be adopted, and let subscription to it on the part of each theological professor be required as an assurance of his entire agreement with its views of doctrine and of his determination to teach fully the truth which it expresses and nothing contrary to its declarations.

It seems to me, gentlemen, that you owe this to yourselves, to your professors, and to the denomination at large; to yourselves, because your position as trustees makes you responsible for the doctrinal opinions of your professors, and the whole history of creeds has proved the difficulty without them of convicting errorists of perversions of the Word of God—to your professors, that their doctrinal sentiments may be known and approved by all, that no charges of heresy may be brought against them; that none shall whisper of peculiar notions which they hold, but that in refutation of all charges they may point to this formulary as one which they hold *ex animo,* and teach in its true import—and to the denomination at large, that they may know in what truths the rising ministry are instructed, may exercise full sympathy with the necessities of the institution, and look with confidence and affection to the pastors who come forth from it.

But some one will object that Scripture authorizes no such test in our churches; and that as Christians, who claim even in matters of church government to be guided merely by Scripture example and precept, the Baptists cannot consistently introduce it. Let the objection be admitted. It would operate only against the use of such tests in a church and not in any voluntary society or combination into which we enter of our own accord. The theological school is not a matter of scriptural regulation, as is the church; and in arranging its laws, we have only to see to it that the principles upon which they are based do not violate those of the Scriptures. They may be matters of mere expediency. The church being a scriptural institution, receives its laws and its forms from the commands or examples contained in the New Testament; but the theological institution receives such laws as human wisdom can best devise, to carry out the laudable designs of its founders.

But I cannot grant that such a test is without due warrant from Scripture, even in the church. The very duties which God enjoins upon the churches plainly suppose the application of every principle involved in the establishment of creeds. They are directed to contend earnestly against error and for the faith once delivered to the saints. They are to mark them which cause divisions and offenses contrary to the doctrine which they have learned. They are to cut off them which trouble them by the proclamation of false doctrine. A man that is an heretic after the first and second admonitions is to be rejected. They are commendable when they try false prophets and pseudo-apostles, and blameworthy whenever teachers of false doctrine are found among them. So far, indeed, did the apostles enjoin the trial and reprobation of men guilty of false doctrine, that the Christian, even in his private capacity, is told that in receiving such an one into his house, or in bidding him Godspeed, he becomes a partaker of his evil deeds.

The obligations, thus, imposed upon Christians involve the decision of what is truth, not merely that they may believe it, but that they may repudiate those that reject it. They compel every man to establish his own standard of biblical doctrine and by it to judge others. He does not obey the apostolic injunction by receiving men simply because they profess to adopt the same canon of Scripture, but by requiring assent also to the particular truths which he knows to be taught therein. It is not whether they believe the Bible, but whether believing it they deduce from it such doctrine as shows, according to the judgment of the Christian, that they have been so taught by the Spirit of God as to be guided into the knowledge of all truth.

The adoption of an abstract of doctrine is but the means taken by the church to meet these obligations. Perceiving the probability that at some time such questions must arise, she acts beforehand, when her judgment is perfectly cool, when there are no outward circumstances to warp it, and when she can patiently examine the Word of God, and know if these things be so. The time of trial is not the time for legislation. Too many evil passions are then awakened, too many unfounded prejudices then excited, to allow that freedom from bias necessary to justice, as well to the purity of the church of Christ, as to the orthodoxy of the member arraigned before it. Matters of doctrine must be arranged beforehand, when God can be approached in prayer, when His Word can be diligently studied, and when the mind is ready to receive the conclusions to which prayer and study may lead.

This development of their necessity leads us naturally to believe that doctrinal confessions were applied to this purpose in the apostolic churches. Accordingly, we find that the germ of them as used for a two-fold purpose, the declaration of faith and the testing of its existence in others, seems traceable to the apostles and even to Christ himself. It is remarkable that it has been so frequently overlooked that, upon almost every approach to Him for the performance of a cure, Christ demanded that public confession of His ability to do so, which involved the confession of His messiahship and divine authority, and manifested the individual approaching Him to be one of those who had been taught by the Spirit. That was a memorable illustration of the same principle, when, after inquiring the views of others, He made a direct appeal to His own disciples, and said—"But whom say ye that I am?" and when Peter answered, "Thou are the Christ, the Son of the living God," in commendation of that declaration, He pronounced him blessed and taught by his Father in heaven. This commendation was given to an express confession of faith. The act of baptism also, enjoined by Christ as the initiative rite of His church, is an act which involves in the very formulary which accompanies it, profession of doctrinal belief.

The idea of a profession of the name and doctrine of Christ, originated by these, and doubtless by many unrecorded circumstances, had in the times of the apostles universally spread. It was then that the confession of doctrine became more particularly the test of pretension to the name of Christian and to the authority of teacher of the Word of God. The gospel which Paul preached, by which is meant the doctrine he had taught them, was to be such a test that he who should speak otherwise was to be regarded as preaching another gospel and was to be accursed. The apostle John, in his first general epistle, charges the churches to try the spirits, whether they be of God, and encourages them to that duty by calling to their remembrance their past victories over error. The confession of that particular doctrine then chiefly denied by the heretics who abounded was the test to be applied. Here it is evident that a general declaration of belief in the truth of the Scriptures, or the authority of the apostles, was not to be deemed sufficient, but a declaration to be made in a form of words which put a particular interpretation upon the Scriptures. "That Jesus Christ is come in the flesh," was required by apostolic command of every teacher of the churches. The allusion made by the author of the Book of Revelation to the relations borne to heretics by the churches to which he wrote, confirms us still more in the opinion that the churches of that day were accustomed to receive a declaration of doctrine, to judge of its purity, to exclude for any defect therein, and that this was done with reference to certain doctrinal sentiments avowed, and not to any denial of a general belief of Scripture.

The same two-fold use of creeds may be traced historically through the fathers of the first three centuries. It is apparent that these formularies of doctrinal confession continued to exist, that they were used at the baptism of Christians, that they were applied to the doctrine of error, that they were of various extent, comprising several doctrines of Christianity, that the doctrines added to those which were fundamental were such as were opposed to the peculiar heresies of the section of country which used them, that they were gradually increased as questions about doctrines multiplied in the churches, and that they were not in the same language, betokening their separate origin in the particular churches which used them. Their use in these centuries, however, is simply valuable as showing the growth and development of a Christian practice already established. It shows the value attached to them by the more immediate successors of the apostles, and as evidencing, by the providence of God, that He intended them, like all other blessings conferred upon the churches, to be continued in use to the remotest ages.

By the Baptists of all ages, creeds have been almost universally used and invariably in this two-fold way. To some of other denominations, it has seemed that we have been without them because the principle of liberty of conscience which we have at the same time maintained has forbidden the laying of civil disabilities upon those who have differed from us. We have appeared to them, therefore, to put them forth only as declarative of our principles. It is to be regretted that many Baptists in our own day have given countenance to this opinion by misstatements of our practice. And it would, therefore, have been to me tonight a pleasant labor to pass over the history of our denomination in the past, in proof of the position we have undoubtedly occupied. But I could not have done this without sacrificing a stronger desire to present to your consideration questions of greater practical utility.

Suffice it to state that we have simply maintained that civil disabilities are not the means of punishing the offending members of the church of Christ. We have looked to the Scriptures for the rule to govern us in such matters, and we have adopted the truly apostolic plan by which we have accomplished all at which they aimed. The truth of God, which we have held, has been plainly declared. A confession of faith in Christ, and in at least the prominent doctrines of Christianity, has been required of the candidate for baptism. By the principles, thus, set forth, we have judged the heretical among us and, wherever they agreed not with us, have excommunicated them from our churches and our fellowship. The ideas which we have held of the spiritual nature of the kingdom of Christ have developed the principle of liberty of conscience and debarred us from the infliction of bodily punishment or the subjection of any civil disability. But the same views of the spirituality of the church have impressed upon us the necessity of excluding those who have violated the simplicity which is in Christ.

It is, therefore, gentlemen, in perfect consistency with the position of Baptists, as well as of Bible Christians, that the test of doctrine I have suggested to you should be adopted. It is based upon principles and practices sanctioned by the authority of Scripture and by the usage of our people. In so doing, you will be acting simply in accordance with propriety and righteousness. You will infringe the rights of no man, and you will secure the rights of those who have established here an instrumentality for the production of a sound ministry. It is no hardship to those who teach here to be called upon to sign the declaration of their principles, for there are fields of usefulness open elsewhere to every man, and none need accept your call who cannot conscientiously sign your formulary. And while all this is true, you will receive by this an assurance that the trust committed to you by the founders is fulfilling in accordance with their wishes, that the ministry that go forth have here learned to distinguish truth from error, and to embrace the former, and that the same precious truths of the Bible which were so dear to the hearts of its founders, and which I trust are equally dear to yours, will be propagated in our churches, giving to them vigor and strength and causing them to flourish by the godly sentiments and emotions they will awaken within them. May God impress you deeply with the responsibility under which you must act in reference to it!

These, gentlemen, are the changes I would propose in theological institutions. To you I submit them as unto wise men; judge ye what I say. I feel confident that I need not ask you to consider them in a spirit of candid inquiry. The very subject with which they are connected commends them to your attention. With such men I feel that appeals are superfluous, and that changes, the scripturalness, practicability and importance of which seems so manifest, will be made the subject of earnest prayer to God for guidance, and will secure your approval and adoption, if that guidance be vouchsafed.

I may be permitted to say, however, that we have reached a crisis in theological education. Some change has become necessary. The dissatisfaction which prevails in the denomination, taking various forms in different individuals, is indicative of the common sentiment that our past efforts have been a failure. Had we labored alone in this cause, I might have believed this due to the want of a sufficiently elevated institution. But the failures of other denominations at whose institutions are pursued as extensive courses of study as can be compressed into three years, and who have in charge of theological education men of preeminent abilities and scholarship, show that the evil rests not entirely here. While, therefore, we seek a change by aiming to establish a common institution, let us see to it that our changes there and elsewhere are not confined to the extended facilities for scholarship we afford. As I have shown you, there are vital interests which in that case would be neglected—interests of ten-fold more importance than the single one the institution would secure.

The changes I propose to you, neglect not these interests, nor the extensive scholarship at which others aim. They present facilities to all of our ministry. They give to every one those facilities he most needs. They offer inducements to secure the utmost progress possible. While they hold forth the possession of adequate scholarship as alone necessary, they contend for the possession of all knowledge as important. They urge upon the student such a consecration of every power to Christ as leads to the attainment of the highest possible learning. They provide the means by which the most extensive acquirements may be attained. They point out work before our thinking and reading men, the accomplishment of which will be of inestimable value of our denomination. They furnish the means for the proper education of our missionaries, giving them the knowledge requisite to establish schools of theology for the native preachers, and to instruct them in the truth at a period when a single error may result in irreparable injury to the progress of pure Christianity. And all of this is to be accomplished, if at any, at the most trifling additional expense, either of time, talent or labor.

The principles upon which these changes are based are undoubtedly scriptural. Indeed, in the first case, and in the last, they are not simply based upon scriptural authority, but upon its injunctions and commands. So far, therefore, we seem to have no liberty to reject them.

The details by which they are to be carried out, it is acknowledged, rest simply upon their applicability to these principles, and the simple manner in which they seek their development. Any improvement here will be hailed as matter of additional advantage, and as cause for great rejoicing. It will be perceived that the great peculiarity of the plans proposed is, that they contemplate gathering all our students into a single institution. The courses of study are all to be pursued conjointly. The several classes of young men are to be thrown together in the pursuit of their respective studies. It is for this, as opposed to any other method, that I would strenuously contend.

The object is not the centralization of power in a single institution, for I believe the adoption of these changes will make many seminaries necessary. I advocate a single one now because the demand for more than one does not exist. But it is that our young men may be brought into closer contact with each other. Various prejudices are arising in our denomination among the various classes of the ministry. This would be my scheme to remove them. The young men should be so mingled together as to cause each class to recognize the value of the others, and thus truly to break down entirely any classification. Those who take the plain English course will see the value of learning in the increased facilities for study it affords to their more favored companions. Those who have this learning will see that many of the other class are their superiors in piety, in devotion to God, in readiness to sacrifice for His cause, in willingness to be counted as nothing, so that Christ may be preached. The recognition of such facts will be mutually beneficial. The less educated ministers will feel that they have the confidence and affection of their brethren; the better educated will known the esteem with which they are regarded, and the bonds of mutual love will yearly grow stronger until we shall see a ministry of different gifts, possessed of extensive attainments, thrown into entirely different positions in the field, yet laboring conjointly, mutually aiding and supporting one another in advancing the kingdom of Christ, in preaching His glorious gospel, in calling forth laborers into His field, and in fostering those influences which shall tend to the education of a sound and practical and able ministry.

On the other hand, let these institutions be separated, and the fate of our theological education is sealed. Jealousies and suspicions will be constantly awakened. The inadequacy of the one and the learning and fancied arrogance of the other will be made the subject of mutual crimination. In some of our churches, prejudices will be excited against our largest and, on that account, our most useful class of ministers. In others, the value of learning will be despised. It will be thought that the mere knowledge of the English Scriptures is alone necessary. Ideas contrary to education of any kind will begin to awaken, and unless the excitement of mutual jealousies, motives most unworthy, should sustain them, the instruction given in either kind of institution will have to be abandoned.

Said I not truly then that we have reached a crisis in theological education? A change is demanded and will certainly be made. But through indiscretion, it may be so made as to lead to the destruction of all our hopes, to the removal of all our present advantages, and to the substitution in their place only of such means of education as shall be mutually subversive. Let us avoid this change, and adopt such an one as shall confine all classes to a single institution. If more than one be found necessary, let them all be conformed to this model. Let thorough training for each class be provided in them; and let us take advantage of the bonds which so strongly bind together fellow students to make the theological institution the means of begetting union, sympathy and love among our widely scattered ministry.

It seems to me, gentlemen, that the opportunity you have to show that this is possible involves you in deep responsibility. The denomination will look to you to meet it. It will feel the momentous interests involved, the dangers which threaten, the advantages which may be gained, and the importance at the juncture of trying an experiment which may be a guide to all future efforts. Let me ask you, gentlemen, to meet all such just expectations by candidly examining the necessity of the changes to which I have referred and the adequacy of the remedies proposed. It is to your wisdom that I have submitted them. To your candor, to your love of truth, to your sense of the value of theological education, I commend them; and should you judge that thus the increase, the knowledge, the power and the soundness of our ministry will be best advanced, I ask you to adopt them.

III
Sermons

1

In the Beginning God

Text: Genesis 1:1

[I am] aware of violating a very common rule as to the text of my sermon, in taking an incomplete clause. But the clause has complete sense and were I to add the other words I should be presenting a different subject, in some respects a more limited one than is given by this portion. I wish to talk not about creation alone, but of all the points involved in the expression "in the beginning God." These words are full of sublimity. I trust I may say something that will show this and lead us in adoring contemplation to meditate upon God.

But even were I a man of strong imagination and gifted with the power of poetic description, I should not venture to exercise such powers in connection with such a theme as God, especially to speak of Him as He was—alone in the universe when all creation was absent and then of the bringing into being the myriad worlds and living creatures of His power.

One is well named on such a point by the great failures even of the great poetic geniuses of our English tongue, to say nothing of others.

Read the address to the Deity of Edward Young, beginning

"O thou whose balance does the mountains reign,"

or his other poem:

"Great system of perfection, Mighty cause
Of causes mighty. Cause uncaused,"

One simple definition like that of the Westminster Assembly lifts us up to as exalted conceptions as are possible.

We feel that we can make but single marks, to stand as symbols of the glory which swells up into our own hearts.

The truth is that in Scripture alone can be found anything that approaches the expressions that burst for utterance from even the most unimaginative.

It is when we read the prayer of Habakkuk the prophet upon Shigionoth

—as found in the third chapter of that prophet—or chant with Moses the Ninetieth Psalm, or listen to the words of Jehovah as he answered Job (thirty-eighth chapter) out of the whirlwind—that we find expressions in some degree worthy to speak of God, His attributes, His greatness, His grandeur, His unchangeable excellence and glory.

This fact is one of the evidences of the inspiration of the Hebrew books which have come to us from a nation, not of more imagination nor of higher culture, nor of equal philosophical power with others.

There is a problem here to solve: How can these have produced such writings? And as we stand in wonder beside the facts, we learn to believe that the only explanation that can be given is that which they themselves affirm—that they have been by inspiration of God.

But I think that an equal proof of inspiration, at least of the words of our text, may be gathered in a simpler manner by an inquiry into the wonderful truths which it expresses or implies.

Is it not true that we find here that which no other people have imagined, and yet that which commends itself as truth at once as soon as suggested.

Let me suggest some points which are expressed or implied.

I. *If God was in the beginning, it follows that the creation around us has come forth by His will and word out of nothing.* The doctrine of creation from nothing is a distinctly Scripture doctrine though, singular to say, it is nowhere expressed in exactly these words.

Psalm 33:[6] "By the word of the Lord were the Heavens made and all the host of them by the breath of His mouth."

John 1:3 declares of the Word, the Son of God, "All things were made by him; and without him was not any thing made that was made."

Hebrews 1:2, referring also to the Son, says "by whom also he made the worlds."

But Hebrews 11:3 is still more explicit: "Through faith we understand that the worlds were framed by the word of God, so that things which are seen were not made of things which do appear."

But this doctrine is plainly taught in all its fullness by this first verse of the first chapter, "In the beginning God."

Not that the word created necessarily implies a creation without materials to work upon. The Hebrew is often used for shaping and forming and, therefore, sometimes has the idea of creation out of preexistent matter.

But this idea is involved in the expression "in the beginning."

For what beginning is here referred to? Evidently a beginning before creation, or at least at the time of creation. For the time of that beginning was the time of the creation of all things—for the heaven and the earth comprise the totality of creation. The first work of that creation was the creation of all matter. Then began the formation process by which animal and vegetable life now evolved or formed out of this preexistent material. The very mention of that formation process shows that the previously mentioned creation was one of the materials from which this formation process was made possible.

The grand truth, therefore, of God as the Creator is revealed in such a way as to show that the creation was not one to which He was impelled by nature but by His will alone.

Had the creation arisen from any necessity in the nature of God, then the creation could not have been in time but must have been eternal. But the text declares it was not in eternity but in the beginning, therefore, not in eternity which has no beginning, but in time which has. Admitting these facts to be so, when did Moses, or anyone else who wrote this chapter, get this idea?

Human philosophy for hundreds of years sought in vain to solve the mystery of creation. Modern philosophy with the guidance of the Scripture before it can present no explanation, certainly can give no better theory than this, and, more than this, can suggest no reasonable objection to it. When did the Jews get it? How came it that this nation alone conceived it? Nay, why was it that at the very beginning of their history it came to them, from a single man, not by the agitated discussions of many persons nor many periods?

II. But another fact is also here involved which displays an equally wonderful statement as to the Divine nature. It is *the Self existence of God that is thus shown to us.*

When we present the argument from causation for the existence of God upon the principle that every effort must have a cause, some have turned with apparent triumph and said, Carry forth your principle to the first cause, and as he is the greatest effect of all so must you present the greatest of causes for his existence.

Our natural and easy reply is that the statement should be in this form. Every effect must have a cause or ground of existence either within or without itself.

We have many illustrations of such key causations. A watch has the cause of its timekeeping within itself, as does a steamship at sea or a fish in the water. Especially so does a man in his walk and talk, in his thought and deed, in his breathing, and reasoning, in innumerable ways.

The difference between this and God is that here it is not the mere self causation as to some one or more acts and thoughts, but as to entire living.

This is what is called self-existence—and this is plainly implied in the text. Thus we are told that in the beginning when creation began, and therefore when the laws of causation first began to work outwardly—God was already existent—as Young explains it: "Of causes mighty, Mighty Cause, Cause uncaused, sole root of nature, that luxuriant growth of God."

Now such a conception of God is found nowhere out of Israel. It was left for one of that people long before any other had thought of such an idea to declare this truth, to tell of one who before all things else were made, Himself existed—making or not to make as He pleased all things else.

III. But still another conception is that of *the Eternity of God.*

Had our author only said that all things were made by God or that at a definite period of time or even some indefinite period God had created the world, we should not find [in] him evidence of the conception of Eternal Existence.

But that which was at the beginning of time could go no further back in time—but must have been either then begun to be, as did creation, or must have lived otherwise than in time. The language therefore involves God's eternity—and God's own Eternity—not that Eternity alone which begins, nor shall be forever nor that which looking back on vast ages of the past stands appalled at the length of the past and imagines an Eternity of continuous duration in the past as it does that in the future.

But here we have true Eternity, Eternity not measured by time, for there was no time—Eternity, therefore which has neither beginning nor end, no yesterday nor tomorrow, but best expressed by us because we cannot comprehend it, as a constant Now.

IV. This involves also *the invisible God.*

V. Also *the Trinity*—The word (*Elohim*) so intimate, though not conclusively. It is more like a name given when the name given is seen at some later time to have been most suitable.

But pass on from this phrase to another where the same language appears: "In the beginning was the Word, and the word was . . . God" (John 1:1). This great Christian doctrine of the Trinity here gains conjunctively the reference in the context to the other person of the trinity.

Such then I, think, are the ideas which lie underneath the language of our text. Perhaps they were not fully comprehended by all those that read; perhaps not by the writer himself. If so, it shows more evidently, their inspiration. For then, whence came this chapter for our text, which is but the beginning of a long paragraph?

Whence came it but from God?

I look back along the ages. It is denied that Moses wrote it. It is pointed out that it is a fragment prefixed to the rest of Genesis as a document already having form.

I am ready to admit it. Back then of Moses, to whom?

Not to the learning of Egypt, for Egypt knows it not.

Some say to Assyria and point out the Chaldean letters of later discovery in which we find similar history to that of Moses.

But of the two writings this is so immeasurably superior as to suggest that it is the original form which these others present a deutero-account.

We look back to a common origin and find that it must have come through Noah, whose descendants would scatter it. And then how sensible does it become. A sublime fragment of the literature of the Antidiluvians preserved from the flood. Knowing its history how must Moses have sung it, and how Noah and his sons amid the raging and the calming nature. But there was nothing to originate this in Noah. And we must go further back and trace it to Adam the head of the race.

It would seem that it might have been his common Sabbath hymn, for he enumerates the work of God and the rest of God—and therefore the Lord sanctified the Sabbath day, etc.

But if composed by Adam, then it must have been in Eden before the sad event of the fall, for no minor key occurs in all this praise.

And still in Adam do we find no special reason for its origin.

It is peculiarly a creation hymn. The angels may have taught it to him, nay, the Lord Himself as they walked in the garden.

But it is a creation hymn and carries us back to that wondrous time of creation when the morning stars sang together—and all the sons of God shouted for joy. A magnificent hymn for such an occasion, and glorious is it that it has come down to us.

We may not believe that we shall learn to sing it when we pass even into the realms of the redeemed—for we shall sing the song of Moses and that of the Lamb, which our grateful hearts shall peel out the song unto Him that hath loved us.

We shall remember that He who is our Savior is not only the Lamb that was slain, but the mighty Son of God, who was in the beginning and was with God, and was God and by whom all things were made and without whom was not any thing made that was made—and that when no man hath seen God, the only begotten Son who is in the bosom of the Father—He hath revealed Him in Himself.

2
"Thus Saith the Lord"

Text: "Thou shalt say unto them, Thus saith the Lord"
(Exek. 2:4).

(An Ordination Sermon)

The present is one of the few occasions when we may speak about preaching, the great work of the ministers of Jesus. Such a theme, though only occasionally suitable, should be full of interest to all men, but especially the people of God. In what way should that work be performed? What constitute the special qualifications for it? How shall it be made most successful? How shall it best secure the blessing of God and aid in the advancement of His kingdom? These are inquiries which, while they may be of more special interest to him who is this day to be inducted in the full office of a minister of Jesus, or even to those whose life-work is the same as his, are not without special claims upon those who are to look to the ministry as one of the highest sources of their instruction and who are required to obey in the gospel those whom God has thus put over them.

A great deal is frequently said as to the ministers suited for our age. Some, in pressing the claims for education and culture, would almost seem to ignore the fact that the centuries that have gone were ages of learning and cultivation. Some, in speaking of the need of preparation to refute the forces antagonistic to Christianity, appear to have forgotten that it has had its conflicts with the enemies of the truth in every cycle of the past. Some, in referring to the antagonism of science, overlook the fact that science, falsely so called, was its opponent even in apostolic times. Some, as they are stirred with emotion at the numerous heresies which surround us, fail to remember that such had their place in the early churches and that, indeed, the wise historian of the churches of Christ can trace each of these heresies to original germs, which were condemned by those who were the first great witnesses of the truth.

The truth is that no one age is so peculiar that the ministry of that age needs to be greatly different from that of any other. The work, like the man, is in all its integrity the same, and he who is well fitted for it in one age and clime would not find himself out of place were he transferred to another. The preaching of God's truth is governed by grand and general principles which are connected with God and man and which must, therefore, be as broad as humanity itself and as the relations sustained by it to God.

Hence, in looking for the embodiment of these principles in some such brief sentence as may serve for my text on this occasion, I have found it not in the pithy utterances of some minister of our own day, nor in the forcible conviction of some one of the leaders of the great Reformation under Luther, nor in the eloquent homilies of the golden-mouthed Chrysostom, nor even in the instruction of the New Testament days, but far back of these, even in the fifth year of the captivity of King Jehoiachim in the land of the Chaldeans and by the river Chebar, in the language of God Himself to His prophet Ezekiel. In these words then spoken will be found embodied those principles which are at the basis of a ministry at once true and successful, because such as God requires and such as He blesses.

Speaking of Israel God says to Ezekiel, "I do send thee unto them; and thou shalt say unto them, Thus saith the Lord God."

The first principle here taught us then is that preaching should be *authoritative*. The preacher speaks for God. It is God that speaks through him. He is God's messenger. He proclaims God's truth. Our Lord Himself hath said of His minister, "He that heareth you heareth me; and he that despiseth you despiseth me; and he that despiseth me despiseth him that sent me" [Luke 10:16]. This was not said to the twelve, but to the seventy and, therefore, is true not of the inspired men unto whom the Lord gave special powers, but of all His ministers who speak His truth and whose words are carried home to the hearts of their hearers by His Spirit.

This authoritative character of the ministry should never be forgotten. The tendency of our times is too much in the direction of such forgetfulness or disbelief. Hence the critical nature of the hearers of the Word. They listen not to God but unto man. They look not at the treasure but at the earthen vessel which contains it. Instead of longing for and seizing upon the message from God's Word, they are engaged in critically examining the form which that message has assumed. To some it is unpleasant because too long; to others uninteresting because too brief. These despise it because it is rude and without the graces of cultured scholarship; those because it appears to them in too stilted dress, and is disfigured by over-ornamentation. It is the man that fills the eyes of almost all. Here and there alone is found one who realizes the great fact that God in His providence and grace has sent a message at that hour to the heart, in which the thirsty soul may find God speaking with authority.

It is a solemn fact to meet as minister and people in the proclamation of God's Word. However much the messenger may be but a man, one who stands to us at other times in the nearest earthly relations, though he may be in no respect better or wiser than ourselves—though, indeed, at other times our positions may be reversed, and we be the preacher and he be the hearer—yet, standing there as God's messenger to deliver to us His message, he is the representative of Christ, and in hearing him we are listening to our Lord. The message of the King may be sent through His humblest subject, but if *His* message, it may be believed and received and rejoiced in with equal joy as though delivered by the proudest noble of the realm; and if despised or refused, it is with equal peril as though uttered by the King Himself.

It is well to remember this. In avoiding the extreme of other ages, which clothed a minister's person with sanctity and exempted him from the control of the civil law, let us not fail to give, not to him but to his message, that reverence to which it is entitled as coming from God. And let the ministers of Christ not fail to exact it. Obedience to the Word should be demanded, obedience that is unquestioning, that is childlike in its readiness; obedience that is exact, which discusses not the propriety of what is required; obedience which is trustful, recognizing that it is God that has spoken to his soul.

It is objected that such obedience cannot be justly demanded, because the Word of God does not come to us through his ministry unmixed with error, as a direct inspiration from Him.

The objection is based upon a misconception of what is demanded. It is not that any doctrine or duty is to be accepted or performed because taught by a minister of God. It is readily admitted that error is thus taught and that oftentimes it is as much the duty of the hearer to reject a message as on another occasion to accept it. The Word of God teaches no such folly as that either a preacher or a mass of preachers, or a church, is to be accepted as the infallible exponent of God's truth. Paul recognizes that the vessel is earthen, so that the excellency of the power may be seen to be of God. He warns his Galatian brethren that though he or an angel from heaven preach any other gospel unto them than that he had preached, he should be accursed. It was said in approbation of the church at Ephesus that they had tried those who had falsely claimed to be apostles and had found them liars.

Surely no one should claim to speak with higher authority than our Lord Himself and His apostles. We are told on more than one occasion that the people were astonished at Christ's speaking because He spoke as one having authority and not as the scribes. Yet Jesus says to the Jews: "Search the Scriptures; for in them ye think ye have eternal life: and they are they which testify of me" [John 5:39]. With whatever authority He spake, accompanied by whatever miracles, He referred them to the Word of God. The Bereans, also, in hearing the apostles, were praised not only because they received the Word with all readiness of mind but also because they searched the Scriptures daily whether those things are so. By so much the more are they who listen to the fallible ministry of our day, bound to bring all that they hear to the touchstone of the Scriptures. But when brought there, and found to be in accord with God's Word, then does the message come with authority, and the messenger must be received as would be God Himself.

That which makes this the more important is that in all the more common teachings of the ministry their hearers have no doubt that they are speaking the Word of God. And hence that Word should be spoken authoritatively as His. Its acceptance should be demanded. The great sin of refusing God should be pressed upon those who do not give heed to it. And they should be warned by the severe punishment of which they are worthy when they treat it with indifference, or even with timid unbelief.

It is needless to say what increased efficiency such preaching would give to God's Word. It is not man only that tells of sin and offers a Savior; not man only that presents promises of acceptance through Christ; not man only that calls his fellows to repentance and trust in Jesus; not many only that invites to a life of full consecration to God, and gives assurances to help in the attempt to lead that life. It is the voice of God—of the living God. It is the invitation of Christ—the ever-present Christ. It is the Holy Ghost whose sword is thus unsheathed to convict of sin, of righteousness and of a judgment to come, so that we may say, without exaggeration, that not more truly did God speak of Christ at His baptism, nor to the apostles at the transfiguration, nor to the Jews at Pentecost, nor to Saul on the way to Damascus, than He is now heard to proclaim His message through the men of like passions with ourselves, through whom even in our day His gospel is preached unto their fellows.

Another element of successful preaching is that it should be *declarative.* It should, for the most part, assert and declare what God has revealed and demand its acceptance as such. It should not present His truth as something which may be questioned or caviled at or reasoned about. It should not place God in the attitude of one who must explain the why, the wherefore, and the how of those things which He teaches, but it must set forth the message of His Word as truth which the infinitely wise and true God has made known and which must be true, nay which are true because thus has God said.

It may be that circumstances may compel the minister to set forth at some time or times the evidences which we have that the Bible is the Word of God. But it is seldom that this would be requisite. Indeed, perhaps never is it best to discuss this point in the pulpit. We have but few who question these points; and we have enough of printed books, and of opportunities for private talk, with which to meet these difficulties.

It may be that it is more frequently necessary to show that the doctrines which we hold are not liable to the objections made against them. But even this would call for but an occasional sermon and that from someone who has some special fitness for such discussion. Almost all the preaching to which we are called is to those who believe the Bible and who will accept its statements more quickly than any arguments which can be presented.

Yet how sadly true is it that a large number of the sermons which we hear are made up of arguments drawn from sources outside of Scripture declaration. To what an extent is the philosophy of religion presented! How frequently do men undertake to show us the reasonableness of Scripture truth. With what niceties of metaphysical distinctions do men attempt to set forth the first principles of our faith. A mere declaration of God is worth it all, not only with the ignorant but also with those most wise and learned.

This is especially true with all the important and fundamental truths of the Bible. These are not so much doctrines as facts—facts which the Scriptures reveal and, to which, upon statement, the mind and heart give assent. God has, in these, made known facts which were otherwise unknown and of them furnishes explanation by the statement of other facts equally unknowable but equally forcing acceptance when revealed. How otherwise could we know of man's present condition, but for the fact of sin and its beginnings which are revealed? How could we explain the delay of God's punishment of sin, but for the purposes of merciful probation which He has made known? How could we know of the possibility of pardon, but for the statement of that fact? How could we learn of Christ, but from revelation? How could we explain the universal rejection of His salvation anterior to God's compelling grace, but for the Word of God? How shall we know God's future purposes, but for His revelation of that future?

Let the Word of God, then, be simply declared, made known, spoken forth and such, and men called upon to receive it as such, and the most effective preaching must be attained. "Thus saith the Lord God" will carry home the truth to those who will be impenetrable to any merely human declaration or argument. Such was the apostolic preaching. Such was the message of the seventy. Such was the bold and simple language of the Baptist. Such is our own language when we shake off the formality of pulpit performances and enter into the earnest work of protracted meetings. Such is the secret of the power of many preachers whose ability is feeble, whose learning is limited, whose statements are common-place, in whom, indeed, few can see the basis of success, but whose power is to be found in the simple assertion of those things which God has said as to sin and salvation. "Thus saith the Lord God" is the watchword of their power, and God blesses their simple declaration of what He has spoken.

The third place involved in the language of our text is that it should be *scriptural.*

The doctrines which are enunciated, and the practices which are enjoined, should be those set forth by God in His Holy Word. We should be able to say, with reference to all our teachings, "Thus saith the Lord God." The limit of our instructions should be the limit of inspired truth.

We have no authority to add; we have no right to take anything away from it. We have no power to modify its teachings in any respect. We must take the pure, simple truth, which is there found, and set it forth, not only as the foundation but as the sum of our teachings. Philosophy may have for us its special charms, and speculation may fascinate us by its bewitching visions, but we have no right to introduce these into the realms of the pure light given by God's truth. The past history of the church, especially in its early ages, is full of warning upon this subject. To such admixture has been due every heresy which has led men away from what God has taught.

We have not even the liberty of supplementing the plain interpretation of that truth by our own conjectures of what must be or what ought to be. It was upon this rock that the Jews were destroyed in their views of the Messiah. We must take God's word as far as it goes and no further. We must mark the boundaries which it places. We must not undertake to pass them. The way beyond may appear to us plain, and yet were we to attempt to tread it we should certainly go astray. We must feel that there is safety only in the paths which God has marked out for us.

Upon this very subject of conjectural interpretation, what warnings have we not had in connection with what is known as science? How frequently have men planted themselves in the past upon positions inferred from the Word of God from which the advancing light of science has driven them, and which have then been seen to have been mere human inferences from very insufficient facts? If our attempted progress beyond God's revelation in such matters has been so easily proved erroneous by the additional light which He has given us through scientific discovery, how strongly should we be impressed with our weakness and blindness and the impossibility of our safely taking a single step in advance beyond what God has plainly taught us in matters which are still less within our ken.

And that which makes this especially a practical point is that almost all the differences in the phases of Christian belief and practice have arisen from the admixture of conjecture and inferences, and additions, to the Word of God. If today all men could sincerely agree to take this simple word as the rule of faith and practice, the days of denominational divisions would be over; the people of God would see eye to eye, and all would dwell together in unity, rejoicing in the simplicity which is in Christ.

Upon each minister of Christ, therefore, devolves a solemn duty to see to it that his preaching is so far Scripture that it shall set forth the doctrines and practices enjoined by God in their pure simplicity. To those who do not thus, the Word of God, in the thirteenth chapter of Ezekiel, sent unto other prophets of Israel, is a solemn warning.

> The word of God came unto me saying, Son of Man, prophesy against the prophets of Israel that prophesy, and say thou unto them that prophesy out of their own hearts, Hear ye the word of the Lord; thus saith the Lord God; Woe unto the foolish prophets, that follow their own spirit, and have seen nothing! . . . They have seen vanity and lying divination, saying, The Lord saith: and the Lord hath not sent them: and they have made others to hope that they would confirm the word. . . . And mind hand shall be upon the prophets that see vanity, and that divine lies: they shall not be in the assembly of my people, neither shall they be written in the writing of the house of Israel, neither shall they enter into the land of Israel; and ye shall know that I am the Lord God. Because, even because they have seduced my people, saying, Peace; and there was no peace; and one built up a wall, and, lo, others daubed it with untempered mortar. . . . So will I break down the wall that ye have daubed with untempered mortar, and bring it down to the ground, so that the foundation thereof shall be discovered, and it shall fall, and ye shall be consumed in the midst thereof: and ye shall know that I am the Lord. (Exek. 13:1-14)

These are but some of the verses of this denunciation of those who use false admixtures in building the walls of Zion. Equally terrible is that from the Book of Revelation:

> If any man shall add unto these things, God shall add unto him the plagues that are written in this book: And if any man shall take away from the words of the book of this prophecy, God shall take away his part out of the book of life, and out of the holy city, and from the things which are written in this book [22:18-19].

I do not present these extracts believing that all who have been guilty of conjectural admixture will be subjected to the punishment here threatened. There are degrees of crime and folly, and God's punishments are meted out according to these degrees. There are many who will build on the true foundation their wood, hay and stubble, and they shall be saved. But the only safeguard against any of the calamities is to cling closely to the Word of God, making no omission nor addition, but simply setting forth that for which we may say, "Thus saith the Lord God."

And that this may be fully accomplished it will be well that the very words of Scripture shall be used whenever it is possible. There is special power in such words; power inherent in them as the inspired language of God; power because of the familiarity which the most of hearers have with them, and power because of their associations with the divine truth which they embody.

I have heard sermons objected to because they contained too much Scripture quotation. It is a good fault, if fault it be, and a very rare one. An objection might much more frequently be drawn from the absence of Scripture. How abundantly did Christ use it. How much of apostolic preaching does it not form. The older English divines, especially the Puritans, were greatly given to it. Bunyan's sermons are almost all Scripture. Perhaps in some of these preachers there may have been excess. But the fault of our day is in the other direction. Yet what force is there not in an apt Scripture quotation? It is like the clinching on the opposite side of a piece of wood of the nail that has been driven into it. It gives authoritative and declarative efficacy of the truth by showing that it is scriptural.

Lastly, our preaching must be *uncompromising.* It is God's Word and not ours. It is His message which He has sent us to deliver. And we dare not vary that message from the instructions we have received. Our message may be unpalatable, but it is God's message of mercy and of warning. If we say peace, peace, when there is no peace, we are lying prophets, who shall be destroyed. We may be charged with bigotry, as indeed must every earnest man, but our bigotry need be only a determination to obey God and witness as to His truth.

There is special need in our day for this uncompromising spirit in speaking for God. Our age is peculiarly latitudinarian. Religious liberty has achieved its supremacy only within the past century, and many of its recent beneficiaries, like others who have been bound in civil serfdom, upon attaining liberty are running into licentiousness. And it is hard to stand against this pressure; yet it is our duty. The cause of truth demands it. Especially should Baptists give true witness upon this point. In the past we have ever maintained liberty of conscience when others have been for restraining it. Now we should still maintain liberty of conscience by showing that we hold to that and not to licentiousness. True liberty of conscience is not affected because one preaches in its proper place the truths which constitute the difference between him and others. He may do this in kindness, in courtesy, in candor, and in charity. He should do it. If he speaks not with this spirit he speaks—the words of God indeed—but with the spirit of Antichrist.

True liberty of conscience is not affected when the lines of separation from others are strictly drawn according to the light of God's Word. If one who has been a member of the church has departed irreclaimably from the faith, he ought to be cut off. But this leaves him still all liberty of conscience to hold his own views, without violating the consciences of others who cannot fellowship those errors.

And so also in the separation of one denomination from others. It is pleasant to dwell together in unity, but it must be in unity and not in discord, or it is no longer pleasant. It is natural to love to extend fraternal courtesies and greetings, but our pleasure must not be sought at the expense of God's truth.

So also it is painful to utter threatenings and denunciation and woe, and I fear so painful that the threatenings of God's Word are not often uttered. Some have learned to believe it best always to speak of a Savior's love, and many regular attendants upon the sanctuary have begun to despise, as rude and unpolished and impolite, and low, and vulgar, and unfashionable, and nauseous, and disgusting, and still others as unwise, and fitted to drive men from the house of God, mere allusions to the hell to which the thousands around us are daily hastening. My brethren, to what are we drifting in these compromises of the truth of God? How solemn upon these very points come the words of the Lord to our prophet, in the third chapter,

> Son of Man, I have made thee a watchman unto the house of Israel: therefore hear the word at my mouth, and give them warning from me. When I say unto the wicked, Thou shalt surely die; and thou givest him not warning, nor speakest to warn the wicked from his wicked way, to save his life; the same wicked man shall die in his iniquity; but his blood will I require at thine hand (Ezek. 3:17-18).

Who shall dare to compromise God's messages of hell under such a threat as this?

Yea, who dares make any compromise on any point whatever, when God has taught him the truth and made him his witness on its behalf?

The mistake is frequently made, and too many give reason for it, that to be uncompromising as to the truth one must have a bitter and sectarian spirit. But this spirit arises from selfish passion and not from love of the truth. Is the Christian missionary filled with such a spirit when he seeks to teach the truth as it is in Jesus to the heathen? Was there bitterness in the heart of Paul when he yearned over Israel that his brethren might be saved? Or was Christ embittered when weeping over Jerusalem? Then need not he who loves and cherishes the truth feel aught but love and vehement desire and yearning over those in error. The real love of the truth and desire to see it triumph is inconsistent with bitterness, but is perfectly consistent with the firm maintenance of it upon all proper occasions. It is because it is God's truth that the disciple so earnestly maintains it and does it too because he knows how valuable it is and how great is the loss of that man who fails to attain it. It is the love he bears to his opponent as well as to the truth itself that makes him the more firm. He has, as he believes, what God has revealed, and he bears and must obey the message of his Lord. "I do send thee unto them; and thou shalt say unto them, Thus saith the Lord God."

The minister who realizes his position must be filled with the true spirit of his office. To him his work is not a formality, nor a profession, nor one in which he is chiefly representing his church or his congregation. He will not enter the pulpit ambitious of fame or courting popular display or rejoicing in the flattery of attendant multitudes; nor is his anxiety about the mere form of his discourse or its literary excellence or the applause with which it is received. His is a more solemn position. He is God's messenger. He is sent to his fellowmen. He feels his own insufficiency for the work. He must cling to God for help, and rest only upon Him.

His message too is a solemn matter. He has a message from God to his fellowmen. By that message he shall bind or shall loose. He is to be a savor of life unto life or of death unto death. He stands between time and eternity. His is a word which God will not let return unto Him void. There is, therefore, no personal pride in the authority with which he speaks for God. The weight of that authority is almost crushing. His heart is filled with tender emotions of pity and love for his hearers, and he lifts up his soul in prayer to God for His guidance and blessing.

Nor will such a one rashly undertakes to deliver a message which he is not personally convinced to be the truth of God. He will aim after all such knowledge of the Word of God as he may obtain in the providence of God and strive not simply to store it in his mind, but to obtain a gracious and spiritual knowledge of it with his heart. Thus will he be fitted in deep conviction of the truth to speak it forth without compromise or addition, declaring what God has said with the authority of one who speaks for God.

3

Christ Receiving and Eating with Sinners

Text: "And the Pharisees and scribes murmured, saying, This man receiveth sinners, and eateth with them" (Luke 15:2).

This man was Jesus. The meaning of His name is Jehovah Savior. The angel Gabriel commanded His mother so to call Him because He should save His people from their sins.

His name was, therefore, an index of His character and work. He came to seek and to save that which was lost. He came to call, not the righteous but sinners to repentance. In His more especial work He was declared by His forerunner to be the Lamb of God which taketh away (or beareth away) the sin of the world. It was by His sacrifice for sin that He made atonement for our sins and met all the demands of the law for our condemnation. It is in the furtherance of this work that as our High Priest He is ever interceding for us with God, praying for us as sinners that God will pardon our sins and remove afar from us our transgressions. It is into our sinful hearts that He sends His Holy Spirit, to change them, to convict of sin, to lead us as sinners to look unto Him for salvation, to teach us that there is nothing in us, but everything in Christ, to enable us to cast away all confidence in our own works or merit as fitness, to rely alone upon Christ's work and His promises, and to trust our whole salvation, beginning and middle and end, entirely into His hands.

Christ deals with us as sinners utterly lost and already condemned and becomes to us a complete Savior in every respect. He is the Jehovah Savior of His sinful people.

But there is a wide step between this position, itself so gracious, and merciful, and that in which our text presents him.

We have not here the mere Savior of sinners but their companion. He is not here exhibited only as dying for man but living with him. The picture presented is not that of the Lamb bearing away the sin of the world, but of the Holy One of God holding fellowship with the worst classes of mankind.

Even our text as translated does not present to us the whole truth. The pious Bonar says with reference to its teaching,

The word "receiveth" is in the original singularly expressive. It means waiteth, watcheth, looks out for, lies in wait. It occurs fourteen times in the New Testament, and in all other places it is translated in some such way: as in Mark 15:43—"who waited for the kingdom of God"; Luke 2:25—"waiting for the consolation of Israel"; Luke 2:3—"looked for redemption in Jerusalem"; Luke 12:30—"men that wait for their Lord"; Acts 23:21—"looking for a promise from thee"; Titus 2:13—"looking for that blessed hope"; Jude 21—"looking for the mercy of our Lord Jesus Christ."

Our text, then, if it presents Christ in His true aspect shows Him to us, as waiting for sinners, looking out for them, longing for them, having that expectation of their coming of which hope is a decided element. And then when these hopes have been fulfilled and they have come to Him, or been found of Him, He is said to take them into intimate fellowship and friendship. "This man receiveth sinners, and eateth with them."

But is this statement of the text correct? It is not Christ that says it. It is not one of his disciples. It is not even the language of the ordinary multitude which surrounded him.

It is an accusation against Him made by the Pharisees. We know that their statements cannot be relied upon.

They hated Jesus and were always on the look out for something wherewith to accuse him. The gospel records evince that they were constant spies upon Him and sought continually to mislead the people about Him. They saw Him cast out devils and said, "He casteth out devils through the prince of the devils." When a man with a withered hand was present they asked Him, "Is it lawful to heal on the sabbath days? that they might accuse him." Luke 6:7 says they "watched him . . . that they might find an accusation against him." When He said to the sick of the palsy, "Thy sins are forgiven thee," they began to reason, saying, "Who is this which speaketh blasphemies?" When He went on the sabbath day to eat bread in the house of one of the chief Pharisees, they watched Him to see if he would heal the man with the dropsy. When He opened the eyes of the man blind from his birth, some of them said, "This man is not of God, because he keepeth not the sabbath day." Thus did they hate and slander Him, and their accusation in the text might have been the result of this hatred.

The whole information we have from the Gospels teaches us to beware how we receive as true the accusations of the Pharisees. And our text is one of these accusations. The Pharisees and scribes murmured and said, "This man receiveth sinners, and eateth with them."

The charge which they made against Jesus was an extraordinary one. His alleged conduct seems greatly to have astonished them. We live at too great a distance of time and under too different circumstances to judge of it. But it was such action as must greatly have perplexed the pious people among the Jews. Here was a religious teacher, one who was declared to be the Messiah, one whose personal purity and sinlessness were asserted by Himself and by His disciples, and whom does He make His companions? The men of authority and position in the nation? The men who were of special purity of life? The Pharisees who were especially the national purists? The scribes who were so intimately associated with the Scriptures of God? No, none of these—not even the men of ordinary purity and morality. But men who were especially recognized as sinners, who were so known as such as to be marked as a special class. And, then, not only these, but even the publicans, the oppressive tax-gatherers, who had sold themselves to the Roman nation and who were enriching themselves by their extortions upon the Jews. These were they whom Jesus is said to have sought after, waited for, expected and longed for as guests, and chosen to sit with Him at table.

Hence the Pharisees immediately seize upon it as a ground of accusation. They show their malice and mischief-making spirit by immediate murmurs. "See what he is doing, this teacher of morals, this Messiah of the Jews, this pretended pure and Holy One. Men are known by the company they keep. See his companions, his chosen ones, whom he delights to honor, whom he eats and drinks with—see him—Why, this man receiveth sinners, and eateth with them."

Is their charge correct?

We look to the record, and we see that the charge is true in all its fullness. At the feast of Matthew, himself a publican, though called as one of the twelve, we are told that "many publicans and sinners came and sat down with him and his disciples." When Christ entered Jericho, He offered Himself as a guest to Zaccheus the chief of the publicans. Indeed, the very occasion of the murmuring of the Pharisees in our text was that all the publicans and sinners draw near unto Christ to hear him, and doubtless the very manner of His reception of them justifies the peculiar word of the accusation which charged Christ as expectantly awaiting them.

At the feast of Matthew, Christ Himself acknowledged that the accusation made at that feast was true and assigned the reason for His conduct. But on that occasion He seems simply to have admitted these sinners as companions. His answer was that He had come to call not the righteous but sinners to repentance. It was, therefore, natural that He should consort with those He came to save. The more wicked they were, the more they needed His salvation. The more steeped in sin, the more call was there for His influence to draw them from it. The more guilty they were, the more did they need encouragement to come to Him. The announcement of the nature of His work was, therefore, an assignment of sufficient reason for His stooping to the very depths of human sin to lift out of its toils and from their own defilement the men who were most deeply stained and most inextricably entangled.

In the light of Christ's life and work as we now see it, we can comprehend the fullness of His mercy and the appropriateness of His action.

He who brings bread to the hungry will seek first those who are ready to perish. Though all may need his help, yet must these first be relieved who otherwise may die before their turn may come.

Such, therefore, was Christ's true and justifying answer to the charge at Matthew's feast that He was consorting with sinners. But, as we have seen, the accusation in our text is stronger. It is not merely companionship where men had come in as these did and sat down at the feast with Him and His disciples. It is more than this that is here implied. It is that Christ was waiting, watching, looking out for, hoping to receive, and expecting with earnest desire that these sinners should come to Him.

And Christ makes to this charge a most remarkable answer, one which shows that we may give to this word "receiveth" all the fullness of meaning which may at any time be ascribed to it.

His answer is contained in three of the most remarkable parables to be found in all His sayings. In them He shows that this is His true attitude, nay, that the word of the accusation does not go far enough. It does not express the full truth. There is must more than any could have imagined from His conduct.

Thus replying, too, He shows us unmistakably that the disposition toward sinners He then sets forth is not that of a transient occasion but the pervading and ruling spirit of His life. Nay, that thus is set forth the grand truth in His spiritual kingdom of the deep yearning which He feels that every sinner, a single sinner though but one, any sinner the more vile he be the more is it true, should find in Him salvation and restoration to the failed relationship of God.

The first parable by which He teaches this is that of the shepherd of an hundred sheep leaving the ninety and nine safe within the fold while he goes forth into the wilderness to seek the one that is lost. How strongly and yet how sweetly does the familiar illustration come home to the hearts of all. The anxiety of the shepherd, the danger of the sheep, his going forth with longing heart into the pathless wilderness to seek the sheep, straying perhaps in indifference, in ignorance of danger, perhaps in joy of forbidden pastures, and the speed which the shepherd makes lest the darkness should overtake him and his search be vain or the cold of the night benumb the straying lamb until it perish or the wolf come and devour it when there is no protector by, and when he finds, how tenderly does he deal with it, not chiding nor chastising, not roughly driving it before him nor even leading it back again over the rough roads, but laying it upon his shoulders, bearing for it all the pain and toil of the return and gladly bearing it because of the joy which he feels that he has recovered his sheep. As we recall the emotions natural to the shepherd, we can imagine that joy with which he makes his voice to ring, over hill and dale, calling out to his friends and neighbors, "I have found my sheep, I have found my sheep! Rejoice with me! I have found my sheep!"

Is it true that Jesus thus yearns over every lost sinner and thus longs to find him and to bring him back into his fold? He tells us so. It is thus that He answers the accusation of the Pharisees that He was an expectant looker-out for sinners, eagerly desires to receive and entertain them. Yes, and He adds that as He thus brings each one by persistence and faith into His kingdom, He shouts out His triumph throughout the realms of heaven, and the angelic hosts rejoice at the salvation of a single man.

> There are ninety and nine that safely lay
> In the shelter of the fold,
> But one had wandered far away
> In the desert so lone and cold
> Away in the mountains wild and bare,
> Away from the Shepherd's tender care.
>
> Shepherd! hast thou not here thy ninety and nine?
> Are they not enough for thee?
> But the Shepherd replied "This one of mine
> has wandered away from me;
> The way may be wild and rough and steep;
> I go to the desert to find my sheep.
>
> But none of the ransomed ever knew
> How deep were the waters crossed;
> Nor how dark was the night the Lord passed thro'
> Ere he found the sheep that was lost.
> Away in the desert he heard its cry
> So feeble and helpless and ready to die.
>
> Shepherd; whence are those blood drops all the way
> Up the mountains rugged track
> They were shed for the one who had gone astray.

> Ere the shepherd could bring him back.
> Lord, why are thy hands so rent and torn
> For him they were pierced with many a thorn.
>
> And afar up the mountain thunder riven
> And along the rocky steep
> There arose the glad song of joy to heaven
> Rejoice, I have found my sheep.
> And the angels echoed around the throne
> Rejoice, for the Lord brings back His own.

This first parable in which He thus replies mingles the idea of compassion for the sheep with that of the loss of something which is owned. Our Lord, therefore, proceeds one step further in the next by the exclusion of the possible suffering of that which was lost. He thus sets before us the fact that His yearning is not simply compassion, but earnest desire to regain a lost possession. It is the parable of the woman who has lost one out of ten pieces of silver. The lost piece cannot suffer. It cannot be destroyed. It will remain as valuable in itself as ever. If found by another, it will be as useful as ever. But it is a lost piece of property. And the woman begins for it a diligent search. Can we not see her as she looks in one possible place and then another? "Where can I have put it?" she exlaims. "Could I have mislaid it, or have I dropped it?" And as she thinks of this possibility, she lights a candle and sweeps the house and seeks diligently until she finds it.

Is this descriptive of Christ? He says it is. He says it to the Pharisees, who have despised Him for His intercourse with sinners. And, thus, He declares to them these sinners are mine. Each one of them is mine. You say that I am waiting for them. I am doing more than this. Your word waiting does not express the idea. I have lost my property, which I would regain for my happiness and joy, and I am searching for it.

How blessed the language, how deeply should it impress every heart: Christ is searching after sinners. He has lighted His candle. He is sweeping the floor. He is determined to find that poor sinner if possible. Who is it that He thus seeks? It is every sinner. It is any sinner. It is the sinner that is most utterly lost. It is the sinner who cannot even move to come unto Him, but upon whom He will throw the light of His candle, and by the reflection of His light from the lost one will recover His own, and replace him in His treasury.

Here again, the joy He asserts as His in such finding. Imagine the woman's exultation after her long and diligent search. She calls to all her friends. "I have found it, I have found it!" And so Christ also has His joy as He sees of the travail of His soul and the angels who strengthened Him in Gethsemane proclaim to the heavenly host the new cause of rejoicing—"Another soul of man is saved. Another penitent is found!"

Ah, but our hearts respond "there is no sin there, no sin in the coin, none even in the sheep even if willfully it had strayed." Doubtless the Pharisees were ready to say the same thing with a sneer. Why talk of such loss and finding in connection with such sinners?

But Christ stopped the sneer of the Pharisees by His third and last parable, that inimitable one of the Prodigal Son. Here there was sin. It was a willful son, one not content with his father's house and love, one anxious to shake off dependence upon that father's authority, one bent upon the free use of all he might call his own, going forth—and that not to a wise but a foolish and sinful use of his opportunities, spending his whole substance in riotous living, brought to a sense of his sinful rebellious and wasted life only by his condition of starvation and servitude, and thus returning. And to such as one how does the father, who here stands for Jesus, appear? As one stern and unbending and unforgiving? turning away in wrath from his spendthrift son and looking with disgust upon his tattered rags? Nay, it is the father who has never forgotten the absent one, who has ever yearned over him, who now sees him while yet afar off, and recognizes him even in his beggary and rags, and who waits not for words of penitence, but filled with compassion runs and falls upon his neck and kisses him, owns him as his son, clothes him with the best robe, putting the ring upon his finger and shoes upon his feet, and kills the fatted calf in honor of his return.

No question here of sinfulness, nor of abundant provocation to anger. But still less question of earnest love and vehement desire to get back the lost one. The parable appeals to every child, and especially to every parent. Can there be such love, such forgiveness, such indestructible compassion. Our hearts say, "yes, yes." They yearn for our own children. We would do all this for them. No joy could exceed the joy which would fill a father's heart at this the safe return of one long mourned as lost.

Christ says, as are your hearts so is mine. It is on this account and with these feelings that I seek after sinners. Each of them is as dear to me as such a son to you. As you feel more tenderly even to the undeserving when lost, than to the dutiful who have never strayed, so do I feel towards my poor lost ones. The more they have strayed, the more do I yearn. The greater the sinner, the more anxious my heart. My love has never failed. I have never forgotten one. And I stand as did the father of the prodigal looking out even into the far distance that I may see the penitent return.

Such then is Christ's answer to the charge of the Pharisees. He uses all three of these parables to explain it. No one of them is sufficient. They must be continued together to teach the whole truth. His enemies said, "He receiveth sinners," He waits for them, watches for them, is expecting them, takes delight in their coming. This was their reproach.

Christ says to them, You have but a part of the truth. I do not only wait, I go and seek the lost, I am filled with anxiety to find my sheep. I search for my treasure as with lighted candle and sweeping broom. My heart yearns for the wanderer, I look eagerly for him, my spirit within cries out in weariness at his delay. I am ready to welcome him with unequalled honors. It is not pleasure only that I take in the society of these sinners. My soul cries out with joy. I cannot contain my feelings. To all my servants around as each returns I impart my rapture, and the heavens ring with joyful exclamation as a single sinner comes back to God.

Do you believe Jesus, my hearers? Has He spoken here the truth concerning Himself? Is it, can it be, true that Jesus thus yearns over each one here? That He thus earnestly desires the salvation of each soul?

Too long have you lingered in the ways of sin and folly. Too long have you stood and trembled and doubted what might be His feelings toward you.

Hearken today to the message of His yearning love by which he would win you.

It tells you of sinners waited for, longed for with deep desire.

It tells you of the yearnings of your Jehovah Savior who cannot afford to lose you. It tells you of His earnest seeking, by which He would take you wounded and sore and unable to return and bear you back upon His shoulders to the fold.

Can you resist these pleadings? Can you reject such love? Can you disappoint such earnest longings and desires?

Will you not welcome to your heart your blessed Lord, your glorious Savior, who thus seeks you that He may regain His wandering sheep, His lost treasure, His prodigal child, that He may once more number you among His own.

Suffer this day the word of exhortation. Would that I could utter such words as would make you hesitate no longer.

Where shall I find them? Isaiah 55:1, "Ho, every one that thirsteth, come ye to the waters, and he that hath no money; come ye, buy, and eat; yea, come, buy wine and milk without money and without price."

4

The Place and Power of Prayer

Text: And this is the confidence that we have in him, that,
if we ask anything according to his will, he heareth us:
And if we know that he hear us, whatsoever we ask,
we know that we have the petitions that we desire of
him (1 John 5:14-15).

This is very confident language of the apostle. Yet is his confidence in no respect misplaced. It is the Son of God, who will thus assuredly hear the prayers of His people. And He it is that said, "Whatsoever ye shall ask in my name, that will I do, that the Father may be glorified in the Son." "If ye shall ask anything in my name, I will do it." Christianity is therefore committed to the power of believing prayer when made in accordance with the will of God.

It is not all prayer that is acceptable before God. The prayers of the wicked are an abomination in His sight. Nor is every prayer of the righteous man one that rises to His throne. "Without faith it is impossible to please him; for he that cometh to God must believe that he is, and that he is a rewarder of them that diligently seek him." Nor this alone, but, to be sure of His blessing we must "ask . . . according to his will." With a spirit submissive unto Him, must we send up our petitions to His throne, knowing that He can best judge what should be granted and what refused. But He hears us, whatsoever we ask, and we have the petitions that we desire of Him, not always in the direct bestowal of these things upon us, but in His granting unto us His most gracious inclinations and devising for us the most truly beneficial blessings, and bestowing or withholding as He sees to be most accordant with blessing to us.

That, under these most just and merciful restrictions, there is a place for prayer the Christian cannot doubt. The Bible enjoins it as a duty and that not simply as worship but as petition unto God. We are to pray for ourselves. We are to pray for others. We must even ask that the will of God be done on earth and that His kingdom may come. We are to be praying always. While we are to be careful for nothing, yet in everything, by prayer and supplication with thanksgiving are our requests to be made known unto God.

These injunctions of Scripture are enforced by the examples of men of faith and prayer set forth for our imitation. Abraham and Moses, David and

Elias, in the days of the older dispensation were men of like passions with ourselves whose prayers were answered by God. Indeed, the whole history of Israel is a record of a people with whose national as well as spiritual life prayer was essentially associated. And the Book of Psalms, the outgrowth of their worship, and of the poetic fire lighted by the intense emotion of spiritual desire, remains today the best expression of the religious life, even of those who have been brought still nearer to God by the higher hopes and the greater spiritual life which Christianity imparts. The forerunner of Christ taught his disciples to pray as were those of our Lord taught also by Himself. Each of these great personages had been announced and born among praying people and surrounded by the very atmosphere of prayer.

The Pentecostal scenes of the newly born church were begun in the midst of prayer. It was by prayer that the Holy Ghost came down, that signs and wonders were wrought, that prison doors were opened. It was in answer to the prayers of Cornelius and Peter that the latter was taught to be a messenger of the gospel to the Gentiles and through prayer that the truth finally spread over the whole Roman Empire. Christianity was founded in prayer. It is especially the religion of prayer. It stands or falls with the doctrine of the power of prayer. And, therefore, by all the evidence that he has that there is truth in his religious faith, does the Christian know that there is power in prayer.

But to all that evidence he can also add a personal experience. His own life of prayer has not been one of unanswered prayer. The conviction has been impressed upon him that God has been with him. He has perceived the wondrous providences by which he has been led. He has realized the straits from which he has been delivered. Unto God has he called out of the depths of affliction, temptation, and despair. And there have been answers to such prayers, such answers as have proved to him a present God, a very present God in time of trouble, by whose right hand he has been upheld and who has led him, though by ways that he knew not unto the attainment of gracious blessings. In some instances direct answers have been given, but as he has looked back, at any time, upon the past of his life he has seen the footprints of that God wiser than himself, who has chosen the path of his servant, who has granted some and denied other requests, so that all things have been made to work together for that servant's good. Can one, with such an experience, doubt the power of prayer, especially too when he perceives the blights of his life to have been the results of those acts where prayer was absent and the blessings of his life united inseparably with those which prayer accompanied?

That which draws a man of such experience the more closely to Christ and Christianity is the faithfulness with which it manifests in Jesus the fact that there is a place for prayer. Here is the witness of the Son of God, testifying in the human nature which he assumed that the true attitude of man toward God is that of prayer and that such prayer has power. Our Lord was preeminently a man of prayer. No personage is so often presented to us in Scripture as engaged in such service.

We read that on one occasion in the morning rising up a great while before day He went out and departed into a solitary place and there prayed. It was in the midst of His popularity at one time when great multitudes came together to hear and to be healed that He withdrew Himself into the wilderness and prayed. Jesus was alone praying when Peter professed "thou art the Christ." It was as He was praying in a certain place that the disciples asked Him to teach them to pray. Just before He walked on the waves He had gone up into a mountain apart to pray. He chose His twelve apostles after He had continued all night in prayer to God. At the time of the transfiguration He had gone on the mount to pray and it was while He prayed that His countenance was altered and His raiment was white and glistening. In the garden of Gethsemane He went aside to pray and found His need so great that He went a second, and yet a third time and being in agony He prayed more earnestly and His sweat was as it were great drops of blood falling down to the ground.

Nor were these prayers for others only. They were probably most frequently for Himself. The number, extent, and fervency of His prayers for Himself are important only as showing the personal need of prayer by perfect humanity even when the humanity is that of the Son of God Himself.

So far as the question arises as to a place for prayer, any prayer of His, for Himself or others, which partakes of the nature of petition, becomes most significant to all who believe Jesus to be the Son of God. Here is the testimony of one who knows, and who by His facts has told us that prayer has its power. Are the purposes of God so fixed that there is no place for prayer? Surely He would know it. Is the destiny of man so arranged that the results of life happen according to God's fixed preordination? Still there must be a place for prayer, for Christ's most earnest cries unto God are made, *and heard,* with reference to that hour unto which He had come by the determinate counsel and foreknowledge by God. Are the laws of creation so unchangeable that God cannot or will not answer prayer? Who could tell us that so well as He who is no less God than man? But, on the contrary, His testimony is for prayer. He prayed Himself. He prayed for His disciples. He prayed for Himself. He taught them to pray. He ordered them to pray. He made all His blessings to depend upon their prayers. He promised them that they should be answered, And, having made His sacrifice on their behalf, He has ascended to heaven and occupies the right hand of God that His prayers may be joined with theirs and suitable answers be infallibly secured.

The truth of Christianity, therefore, is bound up with the doctrine of efficacious prayer. It was the glory of Israel of old that theirs was a worshiping people and a God that could hear and answer prayer. The ancestral name from which they were designated was given to Jacob because he prevailed with God. The prophet taunted the priests of Baal with the inefficiency of their god who could not hear, called they never so loudly unto him. But Christianity has not only a praying people with prevalent supplication, but even the Son of God, addressed in the Second Psalm and told to ask the Father and He will give Him the heathen for His inheritance and the utter most parts of the earth for His possession, even that Son is enthroned at the right hand of God as our High Priest to make intercession and secure infallibly the answers to prayer. And the Holy Ghost, the Comforter, hath come from the Father and the Son that He may dwell in us and teach us how to pray, that through our blessed Lord our prayers may rise as sweet incense to the throne of the living God.

Is it not natural then that the Christian should believe in the power of prayer and cling with earnestness to this precious doctrine? Is it strange that he should be astounded when he hears it even questioned? It was reported that at a meeting of scientists in England it was denied that any evidence exists that prayer has ever produced any effect or contributed towards the production of any event in this world. It is also said that a clergyman of the English church, present on the occasion, declared that if he so believed he would never enter the pulpit or preach another sermon. He was right beyond all question. It is vain for men denying the value of prayer to say that they are not attacking religion. The religious life of man is involved in the power of prayer. If there be no power in prayer Christianity itself is but a delusion.

It is well, therefore, to examine this question and, as in all else, to "be ready always to give an answer to every man that asketh you a reason of the hope that is in you with meekness and fear."

In the beginning it may be well for us to recall the fact that the denial is nothing new. Even the ground upon which it is based, namely the uniformity of the laws of nature, was assigned as early as the time of Job. Indeed, it is referred to as if it were the prevalent objection of his day. In the twenty-first chapter of the book the continued prosperity of the wicked, the fact the all blessings were uniform with them and the righteous is set forth as the reason "they say unto God, Depart from us; for we desire not the knowledge of thy ways. What is the Almighty, that we should serve him? and what profit should we have, if we pray unto Him?"

The people of God have met with it in ages long gone by, and their faith has not been shaken. It may be that at times some trembling saint overcome by the doubts suggested has been led, momentarily, to cry out, "They have taken away my Lord, and I know not where they have laid him." But even then the authoritative voice of the Master has revealed Himself, and the heart of faith responding "Rabboni" has been reassured, and the brow troubled with doubt has been encircled with a glorious halo of confidence and joy.

To say the least of it, this denial of the power of prayer is very un-philosophical on the part of these skeptics, for they are objecting to the reality of facts in a mode of existence of which they have had no experience and of which they are profoundly ignorant.

They delight to point out the folly of those who, while ignorant of the facts developed by any science, presume to dogmatize about it. They are especially bitter against religious men who reject only their theories, or such asserted facts as have not yet been proved. Yet they strangely fail to perceive that they are, in this matter of prayer, questioning the existence of facts to which others testify because those facts are not matters of universal or at least of their own individual experience. If one should go to a chemist and dispute the possibility of the manufacture of ice in a red hot crucible he would only expose his ignorance. The king of Siam who punished his travelled subject who told him he had seen rivers hard enough to support heavy wagon and teams, only showed the bigotry often seen in men of narrow experience. If one who knows nothing of the working of electric telegraphs should think another insane who believes that he has received a message in a few moments from a friend in England or California, the knowing ones would only laugh at his own lack of knowledge. Yet, when men are told by those whose testimony upon all other subjects would be believed that they have found relief in prayer, that they have received answers to prayer, that they have been fully convinced of the manifested presence and communion of God in their spiritual life, the testimony is rejected as the result of falsehood, fanaticism, or delusion.

And upon what ground?

Simply because it is not accordant with the experience of these unbelieving scientific men. We furnish them with sufficient reasons for their lack of such experience. It is not that such power might not be theirs. It is not because it is incompatible with the superior knowledge which they claim to possess. It is not because it is confined to certain classes of men by natural birth or ceremonial manipulation, but because faith and humble submission to the will of God are invariable prerequisites to successful prayer. If they would have a like experience of the power of prayer, they have only to come with these accompaniments and put God to the test.

That when thus tested He is found to display such power and grace we prove to them by thousands of witnesses. Numerous instances of such marked responses have been placed on record. The testimony upon which they are based would stand the most rigid tests of our courts of justice. It is a thousandfold more clear and convincing than multitudes of the undisputed facts of science.

But the infidel scientist will shield himself from our charge of unphilosophical action by declaring that he is governed in his opinion by the uniformity of the laws of nature and their invariable action. He will tell us that in this invariableness is to be found the proof of the existence of forces which act regularly in the same channels, that so fixed is the action then there is no room for any interference therein of any higher power, and that so decided is the testimony thus afforded against such interference that he is authorized to believe and maintain, despite all the testimony to which we have alluded, that there is no power in prayer.

If the question between us involved the possibility of miraculous action on the part of God, I should be prepared to deny the invariableness of these laws and to show that God can interfere and change and set aside this otherwise unchangeable action, as I believe He has actually done in the past. But I propose not to discuss a matter evidently not intended to be brought into the issues now forced upon us. It may be that some prayers are answered only by the miraculous action of God, but this is probably true of only comparatively a few. But under the genuine law of answered prayer, and as to almost all such answers, we are prepared to admit the invariable action of all natural laws and yet to maintain that there is power in prayer and place for prayer in the universe of God.

If there be not, it must be because God cannot act in connection with nature without changing its laws or interfering with their regular operations. There can be no other ground of difficulty presented to the way of the answer of prayer if it be the will of God to hearken to it.

But is it true that God cannot thus act? It seems to me that, in thus assuming, the scientists here also dogmatize quite unphilosophically. What evidence is there against the possibility of such action? What do men know of the ways of this Great Being, who must be so far above us, that they should say that He cannot exercise such control? Has the God of nature banished Himself from her courts? Does He withdraw Himself from all activity in her laws? Has He nothing to do with sustaining their action? or does He simply confine Himself to such sustenation? Is the universe simply a vast machine gifted with perpetual motion and flung out into space, needing no presence of a superintending intelligence? Or does God operate in it and through it and by it to accomplish His wise purposes and to further His own glory?

Upon the one side of these questions stands the Christian believer in prayer and Christian men of science; on the other, the unbelieving scientist. And who can believe that the theory of unbelief is more rational than that of faith?

That there is no impossibility in the way of the Great God accomplishing specific ends in connection with the maintainance of the uniformity of the laws of nature is manifest from the fact that He has conferred upon man the power of doing that very thing which is thus said to be impossible with God. We can form our purposes, we can design that certain things shall be accomplished, we can actually accomplish them; we can thus introduce as it were new elements into the conditions of this world; and cannot God do the same? We are forced to act in accordance with the laws of nature. God thus acts also not of compulsion but of His own will. But the fact that we can thus act and accomplish our specific ends without any alteration of these laws shows to us that the established uniformity of such laws is no proof that God also does not form specific purposes and accomplished by His action the ends which He designs. And if so there is no difficulty in such action on His part as shall in answer to prayer grant the events which are sought by that prayer.

One would think from the objections made to the possibility of such action from God that there is a purely mechanical movement of the material forces of the universe. It might actually be doubted if the presence even of human will is recognized or the existence of mind and of the laws by which the mind itself is governed. But admitting these, how much has not man himself to do with the events which occur amid these uniform laws?

Much that we do is done by cooperation with nature, as when we place the seeds of the field in their appropriate soil and unite with the soil the elements which give it greatest fertility. Thus comes forth by our will an abundant harvest fitted for the sustenance of life, instead of the weeds which would otherwise cumber the growth. In this action we have accomplished a desired end, and yet the uniformity of the laws of nature has been maintained. Why may not God in like manner cooperate with like uniformity of natural law to grant the prayers of His people.

Again, we subordinate nature to our ends still acting under its uniformity of law. I find a tree such as suits me; I cut it into lumber of various sizes and from it build me a house. I have produced something unknown to nature. Yet I have done it entirely with the use of its uniform laws. And why may not God, also, thus subordinate nature to His ends, though its laws still be uniform and its action invariable? Why can there not come forth from the workshop of the Great Artificer new creations of His hands which shall accomplish His ends? And if these be in the realm of renewed spiritual life, if they be sons and daughters born into His kingdom in answer to the prayers of others, what impossibility has been accomplished?

It is our privilege also to supplement nature still acting according to her uniform laws. Our vision is limited; we cannot pierce the heavens and bring distinctly to our sight the stars which form the Milky Way; our sight is too gross and we cannot see the myriads of animalcules which exist around us; and the microscope and the telescope are made and suddenly new worlds of life and motion are revealed to us. Why cannot God also open the eyes of the spiritual mind to perceive the glories of His Word and providence and grace which are hidden to the shortness and grossness of our natural vision? And when in answer to our prayers for the illuminating influences of His Spirit He does this, does He act in greater opposition to the uniformity of the laws He has established than do we in the aids we construct to our natural vision?

We also use nature by leaving her to her course and taking advantage of her unaided and unaffected action. We drink at her springs, we swim her rivers, we sail upon her oceans, we depend upon her rain and sunshine, we breathe her atmosphere, we live in her light. Thus though not acting upon her, we use her in her uniform action. But the God in whom we live and move and have our being, by whose bounteous hand we are supplied, is deemed to have no power thus to bestow the gifts of nature allowed promiscuously to operate to secure His specific ends. Is not the Bible more rational when it tells us that not a sparrow falls to the ground without His knowledge, and when it represents Him as holding all things in His hands, and causing even the sin which He permits, but with which most of all He has had no active connection, to secure in the death of His Son the fulfillment of all the hopes of humanity?

Surely, surely, if we can use nature and it yet remains unchanged, if we can thus accomplish our purposes, if we can thus fulfill the requests of others, there can be nothing in the uniformity of nature's laws which can be interposed between God and the suppliant at His throne. Our unbelieving scientist must find some other ground upon which to attack the power of prayer or to deny that it has its place in the universe of God.

But although it may be admitted that there is nothing in the regular order of the universe which forbids a place for prayer, it may seem to some that there is an obstacle in the fixed will of God ordaining all things that shall come to pass. It may be said that we have only shown that, if God so desire, He may produce specific effects in answer to prayer. But the question still remains, has He the will to do this? Is not His eternal purpose an obstacle to such answers to prayer? And while this question does not naturally arise under the objections of these scientists, inasmuch as it is a real difficulty in the minds of some, I will say a few things in reply.

Those who are troubled with the difficulty will do well to remember that the doctrine of the eternal purpose of God is one of pure revelation. Even the old heathen doctrine of fate is manifestly a corruption of a prior revelation. However it may agree with what nature teaches or reason establishes, still it originates neither with reason nor nature, but comes to us as a doctrine of revelation. And the Scriptures which thus teach are thoroughly committed, as we have before seen, to the fact that there is a place for prayer.

The difficulty, be it also remarked, is not one that affects prayer alone of the acts of men, but it touches their lives in almost every respect. It is at the foundation of almost all the questions concerning the free agency of men. Is it true that man has the liberty of choice, or is he bound by fate so as to be compelled to will as he does in each moment of life? Of the fact of such liberty we have no doubt. We are conscious of it. We can have no firmer conviction of any truth. Yet every volition of ours has been at least so far decided that it has been known by God from the beginning, and either as decreed or permitted, has constituted a part of His eternal purpose fully as much as His own will. So far as we are concerned, each is free; but with God each is fixed. Yet it is still true, as we have before seen, that our volitions have much to do in deciding what shall be the subsequent events of the universe. So also with our actions. In the eternal purpose of God there stand fixed as unchangeably as any act of His all the circumstances of our lives which we labor so hard to achieve or to avert. Before the seed is sown it is already decided that we shall put it in the ground and shall reap from it a definite harvest. Before the city is built it has already been determined that a city shall be at this point, and what shall be its character and size and influence upon the civilization of the world. So true is this that the recent philosophers of the doctrine of probability and chance maintain that the actions and destinies of men taken as a mass may be calculated with arithmetical figures. They even say that there are laws which regulate with exactness those things which are apparently most accidental, the number of murders, of suicides, of railway accidents, of daily railway passengers and anything else which would seem to be most uncaused and least under the influence of laws.

Yet in all these matters who is there that believes that it is the part of wisdom to refuse to act because what shall be done is already fixed? So contrary would this be to experience that all men deride the folly of the man who allows himself to be drifted by fate and uses not his utmost efforts to create the circumstances of his life. We expect no harvest when we plant no grain. No cities arise save by the enterprise, energy, and judgment of their citizens. Not that their destiny is not fixed by God, but that it is so fixed as to be inseparably associated with the use of the means by which the event is through the energy accomplished.

And just as there is a place for the human will as thus expressed in the labor by which we accomplish results, so also is there a place for that will as uttered in prayer by which, as by labor we lay hold upon this energy of God. The fixed will of God is no greater obstacle to the prayer than it is to the labor. Without that labor no such end shall be accomplished as that at which we aim, and without the prayer there shall also be a like absence of the result. The only reason the same principle is plainer as to labor than to prayer is that in labor we can see the force which we exert in cooperation with God, and the connection between it and the result, while in prayer these are hidden from our senses. But we know that the unseen forces of nature are not less real than those that are seen, nor do we believe in them the less. So the prayer which seeks to lay hold upon the strength of God is in its sphere as effective and powerful as the labor which ploughs the fields or the mechanical skill which builds and decorates the cities.

The main fallacy in both the difficulties we have been discussing is the supposition that there must be a change in the acts or the will of God before prayer can be answered. The scientist imagines that for God to answer prayer He must change the course and laws of the universe. The objector upon the ground of eternal purpose supposes that a like change must take place in His will. The truth is that no change is necessary, none in the course of nature, none in the will of God. Yet prayer is heard and has its full place of power. Prayers are themselves means, used voluntarily by us, as we use other means, and used effectively as all labor and learning and skill and judgment, because with them we lay hold, as with these, upon the efficiency of God. There is no change of the laws of nature. None such is necessary to make our labor effective. There is none in the fixed purpose of God. None such is needed to secure His blessing upon the harvest. That we cannot understand or explain how this is true is not surprising. But that there is no absurdity in it, and especially that there is no greater difficulty in connection with prayer than with labor, we can plainly see. In each there is not a change in the divine purpose but only the admission of secondary means, contemplated from the beginning as truly as the result, without which that result cannot be attained, and with which it is distinctly associated.

That this is the Scripture idea of prayer is manifest from the promise to the church of the Redeemer which Isaiah records: "It shall come to pass, that before they call, I will answer; and while they are yet speaking, I will hear" [65:24].

Let us claim the promise made to us in this ancient prophecy, and let us experience the confidence expressed by the apostle in our text. If it were folly, as the psalmist of old declared, for one to cry out in his heart, "No God, no God," still greater folly is it, for man to strive to stifle the convictions which send him as a suppliant to the throne of God. Banish prayer from the universe and you banish God from the hearts of mankind; and with God and prayer depart all virtue, all the foundations of right and wrong and all the supports of obligation and duty. Or, if God remain, but does not answer prayer, what joy or comfort shall we have in Him? Are we afflicted? He does not sympathize. Are we tempted? He does not succor. Do we feel our weakness? There is no strength for us in Him; in our dependence, in Him there is no refuge nor support. We are truly left without God and without hope in the world.

Alas, how little do even praying men value the privilege or realize the power of prayer. Yet no greater evil could happen to us than no longer to be able to look above and say, "Our Father which art in heaven."

5

The Prayers of Christ

Text: And in the morning, rising up a great while before day,
he went out, and departed into a solitary place, and
there prayed (Mark 1:35).

The prayerfulness of Jesus is conspicuously taught in the Gospels. This would be strikingly manifest were we to gather together the many instances in which He is said to have prayed, and especially were we to meditate thoughtfully over the prayers which are recorded. I do not know that this has ever been done. Several books have been written about the miracles which He wrought and the parables which He taught. The Gospel narratives of His life have been frequently studied in order to make of them one harmonious whole; and not content with this, many have undertaken to write His life with all the accessories to the Gospel narratives which great and varied learning has afforded. His teachings have also been separated from His acts and, under the title of the "words of the Lord Jesus," have been learnedly and lovingly discussed in many volumes by the celebrated Rudolph Stier who has even written an additional work on "the words of the risen Saviour." The few but remarkable sayings of Christ while on the cross have formed the subject of many series of sermons. Yet I know of no treatise which has attempted to discuss His prayers, their number, their nature, for whom or for what offered, under what circumstances, and in response to what recognized need.

Yet this is not due to the scantiness of the Scripture statements. They say nothing as to this point before the time of His public life, as, indeed, is true as to almost all else belonging to that period. But from the moment of His baptism the record of His prayers begins and ceases not until it makes known their wonderful culmination in the prayer for His disciples which followed His discourse in the upper room of the last Passover feast, in those for Himself in the agony of Gethsemane, and in that for His enemies while hanging upon the cross.

So frequently, indeed, is He thus presented in the attitude of prayer that we may well believe that it was never absent in any act or at any moment of His life. Our text suggests that pervading need of it which He felt that led Him to rise up a great while before day and to depart into a solitary place for prayer. It is not the only instance in which He sought such protected solitude with God. Just before He walked upon the waves, He had gone up into a mountain apart to pray. He chose His twelve disciples after He had continued all night in prayer to God. Sometimes He would go apart from all the world except the little band of the twelve whom He kept ever near Him. It was thus that He was praying apart when Peter professed, "Thou art the Christ, the Son of the living God." So also with only three of these had He gone upon the mount of transfiguration to pray. It was while He prayed that His countenance was altered and His raiment was white and glistening. These were the same three who were permitted to accompany Him, even still apart from the others of the eleven, when He prayed thrice at Gethsemane.

The record teaches something also as to the nature of these prayers. They were not merely the communings with God of One who walked more intimately with God than Enoch, and who sought the enjoyment of such sweet fellowship and the realization of the outflow of mutual love. Nor were they only those contemplations of God in which was revealed a knowledge more intimate than any which Moses experienced when he besought God to show him His glory. Nor were they limited to that adoration and thanksgiving by which He showed His joy in the will of the Father who had hidden from the wise and prudent the truth which He had revealed unto babes.

They were prayers of petition: for Peter, that though sifted like wheat his faith might not fail; for the twelve, and for all that through this word should believe on Him, that these might be sanctified, that they also might also be one, one in Him as He was in the Father, and might be with Him to behold His glory, and while hanging upon the cross, even for the forgiveness of His enemies.

But the most remarkable fact made know as to the nature of these prayers, and that which is especially worthy of consideration, is that they were most frequently petitions for Himself, by which He sought of God such aid and such blessings as He felt that He personally needed.

It is in the contemplation and study of Christ in this aspect of petitionary prayer on His own behalf that we may learn today some lessons which may be valuable to ourselves. If we can realize the estimate which He, thus, puts upon prayer and the way in which He perceived that it met the wants of His own nature, these facts may increase our own conviction of its value and lead us more frequently and more earnestly to such devotion.

Manifestly our Lord put a high estimate on the value and power of prayer. His professed people may sometimes be very indifferent as to its exercise. But surely He was not. They may lead prayerless lives from which ᴜᴇy are only occasionally awakened by some fearful application in some serious peril. But He was habitually a man of prayer, the earnestness of whose utterances at special moments arose only with that greater intensity due to the greater need. The speculations of men may lead them to question if prayer has any place and power in the providence of God. Daring unbelief may actually assert that it has not and demand proof that it has. But here was one man at least, though through God's mercy and grace He was not alone, who felt its power, who recognized its place and, with the earnestness not of mere belief but of absolute conviction, presented His prayers of petition to God with the assurance that they would be effectual.

Surely the belief and testimony of no one could more certainly attest this power. He is Himself God as well as man and, therefore, knows what power to move God is found in the pleas of an earnest soul. To Him the eternal purpose of God is an open book in which He reads whatsoever shall come to pass, not, indeed, without perceiving the records of His people's purposed prayers, and the inseparable connection of them as of other means in the production of subsequent events. Amid it all He sees the prevalent power of His own prayers which, beginning in the days of His humiliation on His own behalf as well as for His people, have ceased not with His exaltation to glory but continue to be poured forth into the ears of the not unwilling Father while as our High Priest alone He ever liveth to make intercession for us.

Is prayer in vain? Does God mean nothing when He directs that it be offered? Has it power only over the Christian's own heart in some reflex influence that is begotten there? Or does it move God? Does it secure gifts not otherwise attainable? Is it truly a causative means, as are other secondary means, not independent of but subject to the will and power of God? Is it true that results are dependent on prayer as they are upon labor? Can it be that, while the will of God changes not, the free will of man as expressed in prayer enters with real effectiveness into the plans and purposes of the divine will so that with prayer offered something will be accomplished which without that prayer shall never come to pass?

The fact that Jesus prayed answers all these questions. This leaves us unquestionable testimony. To deny it is to deny that He was Son of God and to assert either that He was ignorant of what He was doing and thus self-deceived or that He was willfully deceiving others.

But this very fact of His divine sonship which makes His testimony so valuable presents to us the great difficulty in understanding His own personal need of prayer.

That a man should offer prayer is not a strange thing. Every man owes homage to God. Every man is dependent upon Him. God's hand is full of bounteous blessings which He may bestow. His protecting care may well be sought as a true refuge from danger.

But here is the Son of God to whom the Scriptures ascribe the fullness of the nature of God, and even those attributes of self-existence and eternity which cannot be given to a creature, as well as the omnipresence, omniscience, and omnipotence which render impossible any need of aid or protection or of bestowment of blessing. The petitioner is here petitioning God, yet Himself is God. He earnestly prays as man, yet His prayer is to God and He is God. As divine, He knows all events that will come to pass, yet as human He prays as though He has no such knowledge. The will of the Father and of the Son is the same; yet, here, it is the Son in His human nature that prays the Father. Realizing the incarnation, what need is there for prayer?

It is not safe to assert dogmatically that there is no place for petitions which are purely divine among the persons of the Godhead. Why may there not be petition in some form corresponding to the bestowment of the divine nature by the Father in the begetting of the Son and in the procession of the Spirit?

At least we know that, in His two-fold aspect of God-Man and Messiah, Christ offers petitions and receives gifts from God. We naturally remember here that in the Second Psalm it is the divine Son who as Messiah is told to ask the Father and He will give Him the heathen for His inheritance and the uttermost parts of the earth for His possession [Ps. 2:8]. In like manner also is that most probably a divine or at least messianic act of prayer to which Christ referred when He promised "I will pray the Father, and he shall give you another Comforter" [John 14:16]. Mysterious as may be such divine transactions, we may believe that they are real when separated from all that partakes of the inferiority of the creature and are understood only in that exalted and perfect sense which is also possible with God.

But we cannot find in such possible divine conditions an explanation of the earthly prayers of Jesus. These have all the marks of human prayer, and these marks enter into their essential elements. They are just such prayers as might be offered by a sinless perfect man, convinced of His dependence, conscious of His weakness, overwhelmed with His afflictions, resisting His temptations, and looking upward with earnest solicitude to One believed to be a very present help in time of trouble. Nor can such prayer be accounted for until we accept the plain teaching of Scripture of the full humanity of our Lord. We may find it difficult, even impossible, to comprehend how One who was not only divine as well as human, but in whom the divine nature and the human were united in one person, could have remained unchangeably God by virtue of His divine nature and nothing more than man in His relation to human nature. Yet if we will throw aside our speculative difficulties and accept the plain teaching of God's Word, we cannot for a moment doubt that these things are not only true, but that they could be otherwise.

Whatever, therefore, was the character of the mysterious union of the human and divine natures in the person of the Son of God, His human nature was still left so unaffected by His divine relations that He was in all respects a man, though He was a sinless and perfect one. But this left Him as man liable to all the sinless weakness and infirmities of human nature and to all the conditions of creature by existence. It was as such that He was to live His human life on earth being, thus, as truly a man as though He was not also God.

If so, we can see how He felt the need of prayer for He recognized the weakness of all creaturely existence and its utter dependence upon God. We know of such weakness and dependence from our personal experience, but that personal experience is that of beings still further degraded and weak because of sin. We have been taught it by what we have been told of the fall of Adam and of the angels which kept not their first estate. Even as thus informed, how hard it is to believe that beings created perfect and holy can fall into sin, while cognizant of the presence and observation of the pure and holy God. But Christ realized this for He knew the nature of created mind, the character of the human will and the mode in which it may be influenced for poor or evil, and the utter dependence of every creature for assured perseverance in good in His moral life in the sustaining grace of God as much as upon His power and will in His relations to the physical universe. The human nature which He had assumed was known by the Son of God to be a mere creation of God, exalted, indeed, to high position and dignity by its union with His person yet, withal that, a mere creature and, therefore, subject to the infirmities and conditions of creature existence. Hence His constant prayers to the Father for gracious aid and support that He might finish the work which it was His meat to do.

What a lesson have we here to teach us our dependence upon God and the necessity of constant prayer on our part that we also may be enabled to live before God and to discharge the duties He has enjoined upon us. Each Christian man also enjoys a peculiarly near relation to God. He also is vitally united with Christ. He has been made one with Him but in a much lower sense than was the human nature of the Lord. If Christ in that nature so felt its creaturely dependence as to be led constantly to pray for divine aid how foolish, yea how sinful, is that self confidence which so often leads men to trust in their own powers instead of laying hold with earnestness and faith upon the strength of God. Oh that we could always realize our creature weakness so that being thus weak we might truly become strong in God!

The constancy of Christ's prayers gives further evidence of His conviction of the need of prayer when we remember the especial fitness for His work which He possessed simply as a man. Mention has already been made of His sinlessness, which could be affirmed of no other man except Adam before his fall. But beside this He was peculiarly endowed with the presence and influences of the Holy Spirit. He Himself declared that God gave not the Holy Spirit by measure unto Him. In ancient prophecy Isaiah (11:2) foretold of the rod which should come forth out of the stem of Jesse, that "the spirit of the Lord shall rest upon him, the spirit of wisdom and understanding, the spirit of counsel and might, the spirit of knowledge and of the fear of the Lord." Our Lord Himself declared the fulfillment in the synagogue at Nazareth of another prophecy of the same Isaiah (61:1): "The spirit of the Lord God is upon me; because the Lord hath anointed met to preach good tidings unto the meek." At His baptism the Spirit descended upon Him. By it was He driven into the wilderness to be tempted of the devil, from which temptation He returned in the power of the Spirit into Galilee. Christ declared that He cast out devils by the Spirit of God. No less are His teachings ascribed to the presence of the Holy Spirit, and even the prudent conduct with which He withdrew from the power of the Pharisees and charged silence as to His miraculous healings upon those who were their subjects is spoken of as a fulfillment of that ancient prophecy, "I will put my spirit upon him" (Matt. 12:18).

Yet was it this perfect man, thus without measure endowed with the Spirit, whom we find driven unto God in prayer by the conviction of His own weakness and dependence. How can others hope for any success in leading the divine life who are not only personally so deficient but to such an inferior extent preternaturally endowed?

Our Lord knew that He would not live without the trials and temptations incident to human life.

It might seem that these should be absent from one thus sinless and graciously guarded and guided. But whatever might have been true had He been such a creature merely coming with no special purpose into the world, this was certainly not true of Him who came for the special discharge of the Father's purpose.

He had trials to undergo such as have never been continued in the life of any other man. He endured poverty in that utmost extremity which caused Him to live upon the bounty of others. "He came unto his own, and his own received him not" (John 1:11). He lived a life of loneliness understood by none, without sympathy or appreciation. Even His most cherished disciples lacked spiritual perception and longingly looked for a carnal kingdom. The rulers of His nation, especially the priests of His Father's house and the patriots of His own Israel, were filled with hatred and malice to the extreme of bitterness. Even the common people which once heard Him gladly and greeted with "hallelujah's" His triumphal entry into Jerusalem became the mob which cried out, "Crucify him, crucify him!" Amid such trials, however, there was one sympathizing heart, one ever-present friend, whose ears were constantly opened to His cries, who was always ready to support and strengthen, who at all times knew and loved and was well pleased in Him, and unto whom as the Father, did He the beloved Son look always in these earthly trials; nor failed to find the blessing which he sought.

His too were fierce temptations, real ones, not a mere figment of temptation, but actual real temptation which plied Him vigorously and tried Him sorely. We are told that He was "in all points tempted like as we are, yet without sin" (Heb. 4:15). We cannot measure these words, "in all points." What do they mean? As many *kinds* of temptation in as *many forms* as those of all men? In every kind of temptation that assails His brethren, His brethren who are sinful? What does such language mean? We should hesitate to say. For in both directions we may err. We may suppose temptations dishonouring our Lord, or we may weaken the Scripture statement and rob it of the blessed lesson of sympathy and support which would otherwise come home with sweetest comfort to some suffering soul crushed under the weight of sin, yet which Christ would not break though it be but a bruised reed.

He had to contend with a strong and subtle foe who, beginning from the moment at His baptism that he discovered the relation this new prophet really occupied to God, continued his malignant assaults with intervals only of a season now and then, until the hour of Christ's final triumph. He was the personal agent in the temptations after the baptism. He was doubtless not inactive in those which came through the weakness of human flesh in Gethsemane.

These were all real temptations. Christ is not presented merely in a spectacle or show of what did not occur. As to the latter we are told in Hebrews that there was something which our Lord feared. Let us not attempt too curiously to dig into what it was. It is enough to know that something was feared and that He was heard in what He feared and obtained relief.

How earnest the caution to his disciples, "Watch and pray, that ye enter not into temptation" (Matt. 26:41). He had found relief in prayer. Most earnestly had He sought it. Not once only but thrice had He gone away to God. Whatever might be said of all other temptations, however much we may recognize the self-contained strength with which He parried the attacks of Satan in those after the baptism, in the scene at Gethsemane we see a man convinced of real danger, filled with fearful agony, struggling against some conscious tendency, the spirit willing but the flesh weak, until even His blood was forced through the pores of His skin and like drops of sweat fell upon the ground.

With this spectacle before us let us never for a moment doubt the reality of Christ's temptations, but let us none the less be assured of the power of prayer. It is not here the Word of God which gains the victory as on the former occasion. It is prayer. The cries of apprehension go up to the God that heareth prayer. Again they rise with agony, and almost with despair, and they carry with them prevailing power.

What value have they in themselves? None at all, not even as the prayers of Jesus, but such an inseparable connection has the divine grace established between such prayer and its answer that the one cannot be offered unless the other be attained.

These prayers of Christ which with the Word of God became His conquering power in temptation were not, however, the only ones through which He was enabled to finish the work which He came to do. We have no reason for believing the prayer mentioned in the text as one induced by temptation. It seems to have been especially connected with His work. It was offered in the midst of His greatest popularity when multitudes were seeking Him that they might partake of His healing power and His instructions. He seems to have withdrawn apart that He might talk with God about the work and be better taught as to what it was and might receive new impetus towards its performance, and God's blessing upon His labors. Jesus seems to have constantly delighted in recognizing the relation to the Father which He has as one sent to do His will, to perform His work, to teach His doctrine, to suffer and die as His sacrificial Lamb. When Nicodemus went to Him by night, He proclaimed the wondrous things, that is the heavenly ones, by telling of the Father's love which had led Him to send the Son. To the disciples urging Him, after the conversation with the woman at Sychar, to eat the food they had brought, He said, "My meat is to do the will of him that sent me, and to finish his work" (John 4:34). To the Jews, after the healing of the impotent man at the pool of Siloam, He spoke earnestly of His cooperation with His Father in all His works and declared His own infallible judgment because He sought not His own will but the will of the Father which sent Him.

In like manner does He seem to have associated these prayers with such work. Just before He appointed the twelve, He had spent the night in prayer to God. He commands His disciples to pray the Lord of the harvest for more laborers for the harvest. It was when He had been praying on the mount of transfiguration that Moses and Elias appeared and talked with Him about the decease which He would accomplish at Jerusalem. His last prayer as recorded in the seventeenth chapter of John is almost a continuous talk with God about the work He had done, the disciples He had made, the work He had left for them to do, and an earnest prayer that the Father now in this hour would glorify Himself in Him.

It was thus by prayers of communion with God that Christ was enabled to accomplish His work on earth. As day by day that work had to be performed, so day by day did He seek God's blessing and aid. More especially was this true upon His final journey toward Jerusalem. From that period the cross and its attendant agonies were ever before Him. He talked constantly to His disciples about the decease which He must accomplish there and the nearer the Passover approaches the more especial reference have His prayers to that end.

Thus does He seem to have wrought out His work in His human life through the divine power afforded Him in prayer. He does not put forth divine strength as the Son of God. But it is as man that He calls upon God for aid and receives it according to human conditions.

He has, thus, exhibited to us His confidence in prayer and His conviction of its efficacy, a confidence which failed Him not even at the last moment when He commanded Peter to put up his sword saying, "Thinkest thou that I cannot now pray to my Father, and he shall presently give me more than twelve legions of angels?" (Matt. 26:53).

Thus does the Lord become an example to us in our life work. If we would make it a success we must accompany it with prayer. We can have no more effective nor infallible power. Nothing can be too great to accomplish if we will only pray. No life will be too difficult to lead if we practice habitual prayer.

In no life can we ever live successfully apart from prayer because of our weakness and dependence. Whatever our spiritual endowments, though the Spirit were given us also without measure, still we are not above the necessity of prayer. It is thus only that we can meet the power of the tempter. Thus only that we can live a worthy life in the performance of that work which God has given us to do.

The prayers of Jesus show that those things were all true of Him. They teach us thus the value of prayer, the reality of its power with God, and the necessity of its presence in the life of man.

6

A Christmas Sermon to Children

Text: Ask what I shall give thee (1 Kings 3:5).

I am going to preach you a little sermon tonight—just a little one—such as will suit us little folks exactly. But I do not intend to tell you my text until I have gotten ever so far through with my sermon.

Three or four weeks ago a lady wrote to ask me if I thought it would be right for her to give a book of fairy tales to her little girl. What do you think about it? You almost wonder, don't you, that she was at all in doubt. I did not hesitate at all what to say. I told her to give the child the fairy stories. Why, I can remember very well how when a boy I used to love to read them. I have never seen any harm they have done me. I am only sorry I did not have more of them to read. And I think other little folks are like I was then. I have seen the eyes of the little ones sparkle at the mere idea of hearing or reading one.

I remember that in the fairy books I used to read we were told of fairies who would come to good children and promise them anything they would like to have.

Don't you wish we had some such fairies here tonight. Couldn't we make some improvements upon that tree down stairs?

Yet after all how very foolishly might we make use of such offers of anything we could wish. Not the little children, but even the grown folks are liable to do this.

Remember an old familiar fairy story of a man and his wife to whom, while sitting by the fire place one night, a fairy appeared. She promised to give them the first three things for which they might wish. Scarcely had she said this before she left them to think and wish. They sat puzzled and looked at each other. Then they talked together about the fairy's promise until they were tired. Then they commenced talking about other things. Some recollection of the past led the wife, without thinking of the fairy, to say, "I wish we had one of those nice black puddings we used to have." When suddenly down the chimney came tumbling as fine a one ever they saw! The husband, remembering the fairy's promise, was so angry that one wish had gone, that forgetting that this would be another, he cried, "I wish it was stuck at the end of your nose." No sooner said, than the pudding dangled at the end of the wife's nose. The third wish of necessity was that it should come off again. And so the three wishes which were to make their fortune ended through their folly simply in the possession of one black pudding.

So would it be with us all. We never know what we want, nor how to choose. It is very lucky for the most of little folks especially that they have some one to choose for them. I have never seen it fail that they like what father and mother chooses better than what they would have chosen themselves.

So, after all, if we had the chance we might not make such an improvement on the tree below as we might have thought.

As a matter of course, we all know that there are no such folks as fairies and that there are none of these people who go about giving everybody what they wish.

There is no creature in the world that can do this.

But there was an occasion in which a child (as he calls himself though I rather suspect he was too big to be really one) went to sleep one night and dreamed—and the dream was all true and true. He dreamed that a great and mighty being came to him and said, "Ask what shall I give thee."

And in these words you have the text, for this story is told in the Bible. Can any of you tell where it is? I am pretty sure you cannot. Well, shall I tell you to hunt it up when you get home? I am afraid you will forget to do so. Beside it would be so hard to find it; it is so small a text in such a big book as the Bible. Then we do not treat the grown folks so. We always tell them where the text may be found. Why then should I not tell you? Look then in the Old Testament for two books called Kings. It is in the fifth verse of the third chapter of the first Book of Kings.

Now having stated the text, let me say that I am half through my sermon.

I repeat the words of it. "Ask what I shall give thee."

I. *Who is this that speaks these words?*

It is God, who is a real being, not a mere fancy as are the fairies, but a real being. God, who is able to give you all you ask, whatever that may be, God who makes to every one of us as He did in the dream to this [one], the promise of what we wish. But it is God who will not give us just any foolish request which may pop into our minds or out of our mouths, as in the case of the fairy and the black pudding, but who watches our requests, and sees what we really need and gives us always exactly what is best for us. And God, too, who comes to us in His promise in something more certain than a dream, even in His Bible and through His own Son.

II. *Now to whom did God say, "Ask what I shall give thee?"*

It was to Solomon, the young son of David, whose father had lately died and left him king over Israel.

You would say, Why! He has all things already, no need to give him anything more. He is young and handsome and learned and rich and powerful and a king! What more does he want?

God comes and asks him that Solomon may show all that was in his mind. And now notice his reply.

III. *What do you think he asked for?*

Was it riches or power or long life for himself or evil to his enemies? None of these. He asks for wisdom that he may know what is best and right to do. He is going to have a great deal of trouble in managing his kingdom. He will often be very much puzzled as to what is best to be done. The happiness of very many people will depend upon his acting wisely. He will frequently have to decide as to the right of his subjects. Evidently he had been thinking about these things before God comes to Him in the dream. And hence he asks God for wisdom.

IV. *Now what do you suppose God thought about this choice?*

The Bible says He liked it very much and that He told Solomon so. God told him that He was pleased because he did not ask for riches and honor. And that on that account he would give him these beyond any king of his day. And, that he would so grant his prayer for *wisdom,* that there should be none before or after him that should be as wise. And then he told him that if he would be constant in his obedience as was his father, David, he should live a long life. This was granting his request abundantly, giving him much more than he had asked for.

V. *Now what do you suppose there was in Solomon's request for wisdom that pleased God so much?*

One thing we are sure was because wisdom is itself better than riches or honor or even a long life, and God was pleased to see that Solomon knew this and chose wisdom.

But besides this, this choice of Solomon showed at least three good traits of character in himself.

One was a love of doing justice to those he was to rule over. He wished to do what was right and to wrong no man.

Another was his unselfishness. He chose what was good for his people, not for himself. He was asking for himself as king and not as a man.

The third was his humility and sense of his unfitness without God's help for his high position. Many a one would have been puffed up by the fact that he was king and would have regarded his people as made only for him and cared little for their welfare and felt nobody equal to himself. It was because Solomon's wish showed that he did not feel so that God praised and blessed him.

Now suppose that God should say to each of you here tonight, "Ask what I shall give thee."

Do you think you could make a good choice?

Suppose that you could now while sitting in your seats choose what you shall have when you go down stairs and know that you will get it.

Even in such a matter as that do you think you would make a wise choice?

I doubt it very much. I think it would only be another foolish choice like those about the black pudding.

Therefore, as to this gift God has chosen for you: He has sent each of you a gift, the very same gift to each one of you, which you may have if you wish it.

Shall I tell you about it? It is something that every one of you needs very much. You need it every day. If you accept it, it will make you almost perfectly happy.

It is something too that has cost God a great deal. No one else is rich enough to buy it. He gives it to you though it cost more than all the gold and silver and diamonds and precious stones in the world.

He sends it "with His best love." You know how those who love us write upon the gifts they give, "with best love." So does God and the very gift shows that He means "His best love."

It is something too that is like what is called a charm. It will protect you against all evil.

It is also a talisman like that wonderful lamp or ring of Aladdin which will get for you all other blessings—even those which are most wonderful. So that if you have it you shall live in "a city" of "pure gold, like unto clear glass," the very foundations of which shall sparkle with all kinds of jewels, every gate of which shall be composed of a single pearl, and even the streets you shall walk on shall be of pure gold. The palace of Aladdin was nothing like as beautiful as your home in that city.

Then too this gift shall never be taken from you, nor lost. It shall never be spoilt. You will never become tired of it. Even when you die you shall carry it with you, or rather it will carry you into heaven and make you happy there forever and ever.

It was at the real Christmas time that God gave it to the world. And it is that gift which has made even the Christmas we celebrate so happy and joyous.

Can you tell me what this gift of God is? Can you not guess what it is from what I have said?

It is—shall I tell you—or shall I leave you to guess it, or to ask others what it is? It is—the Bible, you will say. No, it is not the Bible, although the Bible teaches you all we know about it.

I shall give you this clue to it, and you must either find out for yourself or ask your parents or Sunday School teacher.

It is a person who was born on the first Christmas night and the Bible calls Him "God's unspeakable gift."

7

The Uses and Doctrine of the Sanctuary, Making Sacred Our Houses of Worship*

Text: Lord, I have loved the habitation of thy house, and the place where thine honour dwelleth (Ps. 26:8).

It is eminently fit that we enter not this building without recognizing the occasion as one of more than ordinary interest. To the general reasons pertinent to the opening of any house of worship, special ones are here to be added as to why we should acknowledge the hand of God in its erection, should offer Him all praise for its completion, and dedicate it with more than ordinary fervor to His worship.

Nearly a quarter of a century has elapsed since the conviction of the need of a better building than the one we have now left led to efforts to secure it. These, however, were frustrated by the casualties of the day. A renewal of the attempt made twelve years ago also came to naught, though for reasons of a different character. Even in this effort, the successful result of which we this day witness, disappointment and delay and the mysterious dealings of God's providence have often so retarded the work, that we have almost despaired of its completion. The history of this building, extending over a period of eight years from its inception, has been one of sacrifice and toil and pain, the extent of which can never be realized by any save those who have been actively engaged in its erection. God has now mercifully granted all of your desires, and, with hearts full of gratitude and praise for His mercy, we proceed to dedicate to His own worship and praise, the house He has permitted us to erect.

The people of God have ever loved the temples of His praise. The psalmist teaches us how the hearts of Israel burned for the Temple, how blessed they were considered who dwelt within its courts; so that, to be a door-keeper in the house of God, was better than to dwell in the tents of wickedness, one day in them being better than a thousand.

And the language he uses has always been the language of the saints. Whether it be an Anna, serving God with fastings and prayer night and day in the Temple, or one of the disciples of the risen Savior, awaiting at Jerusalem the manifestation of the Spirit, i.e. whether the meeting-place be among the intricate catacombs of Rome or within the rude structures of hewn logs in the pathless forest; whether the people assemble in a cave of the mountain, avoiding the fires enkindled by those who assume the Christian name, or as we today, in a house erected especially for worship, surrounded by every protection which can secure religious liberty, everywhere, for every heart the prevailing sentiment bursts forth—"How amiable are thy tabernacles, O Lord of hosts! My soul longeth, yea, even fainteth for the courts of the Lord: my heart and my flesh crieth out for the living God" (Ps. 84:1-2).

There are two extremes of opinion to be avoided, concerning the sacredness of these houses of worship, one may be called the sacraments extreme, the other, a term which most exactly, though too harshly, expresses it, the sacrilegious. The former of these attaches sanctity to the building because of ceremonial consecration. The other seeks to divest it of all sacredness whatever. The tendency of the Baptist denomination is to the latter. It is as the result of this that our churches are open as public halls for orations before benevolent societies, or on patriotic occasions, and for various other purposes of public interest. The desecration consists not in any injury which the place may sustain, which renders it unfit for the purposes of worship, but in the destruction of those holy associations which exist in connection with it in the minds of those who worship there.

In protesting against one of these extremes, we have too frequently allowed ourselves to run into the other. And it is time, for the sake of religious taste, and the sacredness of Christian worship, that the voices of the churches should be raised against this desecration of the objects for which their houses of worship have been built, and of the religious associations with which they are connected.

The sentiments I have quoted from the psalmist have nothing in common with either of these extremes. The Scriptures never allude again to the dedication services of the tabernacle, or even of the Temple. Those services were, in both cases, performed by laymen, who had no authority to bless. That of the tabernacle seems to have been an occasion for the presentation of free-will offerings by the princes of the children of Israel, by whom it was thus dedicated; that of the Temple, merely the laying of the offering at the feet of God, by him whom he had permitted to build it, accompanied by earnest prayers for blessings upon the nation in connection with it. To neither of these occasions, however, do the Scriptures again refer, yet the sacredness of the place is constantly avowed. The use to which it was put, and the doctrines which God taught by its presence, are made reasons for the sacred affection so constantly displayed towards it. The psalmist tells us that he loved the courts of God because the Lord God is a sun and a shield—the Lord will give grace and glory. "One thing," says he again, "one thing have I desired of the Lord, that I will seek after; that I may dwell in the house of the Lord all the days of my life, to behold the beauty of the Lord, and to inquire in his temple" (Ps. 27:4). And, again, "We have thought of thy loving-kindness, O God, in the midst of thy temple" (Ps. 48:9). The sacredness of the Temple arose from its uses and its instructions; and the extent of that sacredness is manifest, from the remarkable conduct of our Savior on one occasion, and from the reason He assigned for it. "Jesus went into the temple of God, and cast out all them that sold and bought in the temple, and overthrew the tables of the moneychangers, and the seats of them that sold doves, and said unto them, It is written, My house shall be called the house of prayer; but ye have made it a den of thieves" (Matt. 21:12-13).

The tabernacle and Temple were, therefore, sacred places, not because of any consecrating ceremonies, but because of the use to which they were put and the revelations of truth which God made through them to His people. And, in like manner, we may find, in the use to which we put our houses of worship, and in the instruction which they are also fitted to impart, in their simple existence, reason for the exercise of such affections as shall regard them also sacred and separate them from all other purposes than those for which they are designed.

I. *Surely the use to which this sanctuary will be put are sufficient to awaken these emotions in the minds of all.*

It is to be a place to worship God. Here the whole congregation shall unite in prayer and praise. The penitent shall here draw nigh, confessing his guilt. The pardoned will here give utterance to his exceeding joy. The broken-hearted shall here seek the healing of his wounds. Hence shall arise from trembling lips the voice of adoration. Hence shall burst forth the songs of thanksgiving. For it is here, even here, that shall be worshiped the God—the great God, who alone is great—the God of infinite holiness, majesty, and power, yet the God of grace and supplication, who even inhabiteth the praises of Israel.

It is to be a place in which the Word of God will be authoritatively dispensed. Here the story of the cross will move, again and again, as it has moved, the heart of man. The common salvation will here be preached. The words of invitation and entreaty will here make eloquent the ambassador of Christ. Here, also, shall be heard God's solemn threatenings; here shall be lifted up the voice of warning and exhortation. The saints of God shall come here to be fed with the gracious doctrines of His Word, that new hope may be awakened, that new life may be breathed into them, that their stumbling steps may be placed upon a sure place, that their declining zeal may glow with yet purer fire that they may, by the means of grace, become more and more meet for the inheritance above.

The Holy Ghost will here be poured forth upon the individual and the assembly. The worshipers of God will here be taught the petitions which should arise from their hearts and induced to worship in spirit and truth. The preached word will here be made effectual, his portion in due season being applied to each. And here shall be wrought out those greater works than Jesus did, in which men shall be delivered from the power of Satan and sin, and those dead in trespasses and sins shall be regenerated and sanctified and saved.

Here, also, shall be solemnized the ordinances which Christ has established. The willing convert will profess his trust in Christ by following Him into the baptismal waters, and thence, having been baptized into His death, and, therefore, buried with Him by baptism into death, go forth to live in newness of life. Here, also, His people shall feed upon the memorials of the love of Jesus, while they mourn their own unworthiness and wonder at His grace.

This house is to be the home of a Christian church, in which the members shall take counsel together as to the interests of the Redeemer's kingdom, shall comfort each other amid the trials of the Christian life, shall rejoice together in the progress of Christ's cause in their own hearts, and in the hearts of others, shall rejoice in the sure promise of Christ's final and speedy triumph, and shall urge each other forward to earnest exertions in His cause.

It is to be especially the home of a Baptist church, the members of which have associated themselves together in the firm conviction of the truth of the distinctive doctrines and practices of that people and are earnestly desirous so to exhibit these peculiarities as to commend the simple truth in Jesus to their fellowmen.

What sacred associations are thus clustered around the building which we this day dedicate to the service of God! In what sense could the pious Jew find more to revere in the tabernacle or the Temple? The God whom we worship appears even more fearful in praise—more glorious in holiness. The truth which His messenger will proclaim here is more plainly revealed and more manifestly precious in its tidings of mercy. The shekinah is, indeed, wanting, but we live in the days of the Spirit. We have heard of the incarnation of Jesus, and we here find, through the teachings of the Spirit, in the bread and in the wine, symbols of a still more glorious manifestation. With all its glory, the Jewish Temple, with its mysteries, its restraints, and its burdensome ceremonies, presents the marks of an imperfect dispensation, while the Christian church, with its simple worship, the direct access to God which it proclaims, and its offers of free grace, presents to us a perfection, only tarnished by the weakness and sinfulness of its worshipers.

Let the associations around this building be ever of a sacred character. We ask no consecrating waters to save it from defilement. We desire with no measured tread to surround its walls, and thus to render them sacred from the contact of things common or profane. In the services of today we find no stronger power than is to be found in those of future occasions. It is to the simple worship of God, rendering sacred these walls by its blessed associations, that we look for their protection—to that worship, not as performed upon one occasion, but upon all occasions, to that worship, in all its forms, in the act of prayer, and in the meditation upon the Word of God, and in the communion of the body and blood of Christ, to that worship, endearing these walls by sacred associations and not by superstitious reverence. The use to which the sanctuary is applied will fill the hearts of all with sacred love for the place in which they are wont to gather for the worship of God.

II. The language of our text is remarkable because of the terms which the psalmist applies to the House of God—"the habitation of thy house, and the place where thine honour dwelleth." This language suggests, as another reason of his love for the sanctuary, the truths which, either directly or symbolically, were taught by its existence. For the want of a better term, I will call this THE DOCTRINE OF THE SANCTUARY. *In that doctrine may also be found additional reasons for exercising sacred affection towards our houses of worship.*

In speaking of the doctrine of the sanctuary, I must not be misunderstood, however, as endorsing, in any respect, the system of Ecclesiologists. The development of the thought I am about to present will show that there is an essential difference. There is this point in common, that the church-building itself conveys religious thought to the mind of the pious believer in Jesus. In Ecclesiology, however, these ideas are associated with the form and structure of the building: in the other, with the truth which God conveyed at first, either directly or symbolically, by the tabernacle and Temple, and now conveys through their similar objects by houses created for His in-dwelling.

The doctrine of the sanctuary, in its simple form, was declared by God, when He directed Moses to erect the tabernacle. "Let them make me a sanctuary; that I may dwell among them" (Ex. 25:8). The object of the tabernacle was not simply to furnish a place at which the worshipers should assemble, but one in which God should be manifest, dwelling among them as their protector, and the object of the worship. The truth, therefore, which it plainly revealed was, that *God dwells among men, seeking and requiring their worship.* Throughout the Jewish history, this idea seems to have been the prominent one. It was attached to the Temple, as well as to the tabernacle; and, as though to show that it was not due simply to the shekinah, it is connected with the second Temple as well as with the first.

In this simple form, at least, this doctrine has ever been attached to the temples erected to God, (even natural religion, or earlier tradition, taught it to the pagan world). Wherever a building for the worship of God has been erected, it has been a monument to the fact that God does not withdraw Himself from human observation, that His government does not permit the idea of separation in His being from the creatures to whom He has given life, but that He calls upon all to worship Him and is everywhere present to receive that homage.

Our Christian houses of worship have, indeed, only a wider significance than their prototype of the tabernacle; that spoke simply of God's indwelling to receive, at that spot, the worship of His people. It told of the presence in the religious assembly only of the great Preserver and Benefactor—the adorable Creator of all. It confined Him to the locality of its presence. And when the Temple was erected upon Mount Zion, the spirit of local manifestation was only made more significant. The Jew needed to go up to the Temple to pray. In a distant land his face must be turned toward Jerusalem and Mount Zion. It was there that God had recorded His name. He dwelt, indeed, on earth, but only on one spot of earth, nearer, indeed, than in heaven, because more distinctly manifest to men, but still, as it were, inaccessible, hidden behind the veil, to be approached only with awe and reverence, as to the Great Holy One of Israel.

But the temples of Christian worship, while they still speak of the indwelling God to be worshiped, proclaim to us this blessed truth, that in no particular locality alone, neither on Mount Gerizim, nor yet at Jerusalem only, do we worship the Father. The nearness of access by which we cry *Abba* Father is accompanied by the presence and in-dwelling of God everywhere with man. It is not the God of Sinai whom we are to approach, surrounded by His majesty, but the Father, whom we have known through the Son. His special presence is not confined to his temples, but is everywhere manifest. When we enter into the closet and shut the door and pray to the Father, which is in secret, we find Him present to reward. If we assemble around the family altar, God is there. If we enter into the busy walks of life, we still carry Him with us there, so that in the spirit, not of a guilty conscience, but of joyful thanksgiving for such favor, we can appropriate the words of the psalmist: "Wither shall I go from thy spirit? or whither shall I flee from thy presence? If I ascend up into heaven, thou art there: if I make my bed in hell, behold, thou art there. If I take the wings of the morning, and dwell in the uttermost parts of the sea; even there shall thy hand lead me, and thy right hand shall hold me" (Ps. 139:7-10).

With this lesson of the universal presence of God with the worshiper, Christianity, however, unites an especial promise of blessing to social worship, particularly in the organized assembly. I say particularly in the organized assembly because it was in immediate connection with directions about the *discipline* of private offences by the organized church that Christ added the promise—"If two of you shall agree on earth as touching any thing that they shall ask, it shall be done for them of my Father which is in heaven. For where two or three are gathered together in my name, there am I in the midst of them" (Matt. 18:19-20). It is on this account that the building set apart for the use of an organized Christian church becomes the index, in the highest degree, of the indwelling of God with man. It is so, not, indeed, from anything in its structure, not because of any peculiar sanctity to be attached to a particular spot, not from any ceremonial sacredness arising from purifying rites, but because it is the place in which an organized church is accustomed to assemble, and to seek from Jesus the fulfillment of the promise of His special blessing. It is made, by this, peculiarly the dwelling place of God, and, therefore, stands forth prominently as an index of that doctrine.

Any house of worship, therefore, is invested with peculiar interest. Its construction may be plain, its materials may be of the most ordinary kind, or it may awaken admiration by its magnificence, by its exquisite symmetry, or by its elaborate workmanship. Above all of these, the pious heart will recognize in the doctrine of God's indwelling, which it proclaims, a sublimity, an excitement of devotion, a cause for wonder, gratitude, and love, which is based upon that doctrine as the essential, to which the structure itself becomes the mere accident of form. Such have ever been the feelings awakened where the special manifestation of God has been felt. Jacob, as he arose from his couch of blessed dreams, exclaimed: "Surely the Lord is in this place; and I knew it not. . . . How dreadful is this place! This is none other but the house of God, and this is the gate of heaven" (Gen. 28:16-17). Solomon was moved by it to emotions of praise, when, in the dedication of the temple he exclaimed, "But will God indeed dwell on the earth? behold, the heaven and the heaven of heavens cannot contain thee; how much less this house that I have builded?" (1 Kings 8:27). It is the language of every one who realizes the distance between sinful man and the Holy God, the language, however, of astonishment, not mingled with unbelief, but with humble trust, gratitude, and love.

It is OUR sentiments today as we set apart this house for the special dwelling-place of God. We wonder at and praise His condescension; we humbly trust His blessed promise; we look for the gracious manifestations of His presence; nay, we believe that already has He entered this place with this worshiping assembly, to receive our praise, to grant our prayers, to pour upon us His blessing, to dwell in the midst of this people as the God of His church. It is that He may confer these blessings that this house has been erected. Let it ever be sacred as His dwelling-place in the organized assembly; and let us, uninterruptedly, proclaim the truth that God thus condescends to inhabit the praises of Israel.

The doctrine to which I have thus referred is but the germ of more mighty truths revealed to us in the Word of God. The indwelling of God with man, naturally reminds us of His indwelling in the person of a man in the incarnation of our Lord Jesus Christ. The sanctuary of old was intended, symbolically, to make known this truth. And the sanctuaries of the present day, from the similar instructions which they gave, relative to the indwelling of God, are fitted to remind us of it. It seems to have been the plain purpose of God to teach by the Temple the future wonders of His grace. As the shekinah dwelt in the Temple, so was the Deity to dwell in the human nature of Jesus. This point is plain to us, with the light which the New Testament has thrown upon it. It seems hardly questionable, however, that it was known to many among the Jews. Those of them who, by the instructions of the Spirit, had learned their need of a Savior, who had thus been led to feel that there was not sufficient atonement in the sacrificial offerings of the Mosaic ceremony; those of them who, by their meditations upon the prophecies, had been able to perceive that thecoming Messiah was to be the Mighty God, and yet a man of sorrows, and acquainted with grief, with whose stripes they were healed; those must have learned that the Deity would dwell in humanity, attaching to it His own glory, as did the shekinah to the Temple, and securing an inestimable value for its acts of obedience and suffering.

That this lesson was taught distinctly enough to be realized, is plain, for the use which Christ made of this doctrine, in predicting His death and resurrection—"Destroy this temple, and in three days I will raise it up." That it was realized, at least by some of the Jews, is evident, from the attempt to prove Christ guilty of blasphemy, at the judgment, as well as from the language of derision while He hung upon the cross. At the judgment, there came two false witnesses, who said: "We heard him say, I will destroy this temple that is made with hands, and within three days I will build another made without hands. And the high priest stood up in the midst, and asked Jesus, saying, Answerest thou nothing? what is it which these witness against Thee? But he held his peace, and answered nothing. Again the high priest asked him, and said unto him, Art thou the Christ, the Son of the Blessed?" (Mk. 14:58,60–61). What significance had this question in connection with the accusation against Him? So, also, at the time of His crucifixion, they that passed by reviled Him, wagging their heads, and saying, "Thou that destroyest the temple, and buildest it in three days, save thyself and come down from the cross" (Mk. 15:29-30). The allusion here was manifestly not simply to the power Christ would possess, as the Son of God, but to that power in connection with His declaration, that He could rebuiled the Temple which they were destroying.

If we grant, however, that this mystery was entirely concealed from those before Christ's death, it must certainly be admitted that now that Christ has arisen from the dead, all know the meaning of this prediction, and the important doctrine assumed in it of the indwelling of God. The divinity of our Savior is established. The fact that He assumed our nature is perceived. The indwelling of God in man is, therefore, seen, and the language of the Savior becomes intelligible, as we recognize the type of the temple fulfilled in the antitype, the incarnate Son of God.

Nor are these suggestions associated simply with the sanctuaries of old. The doctrine taught by the in-dwelling of God made *them prophetic* of the incarnation of Christ. The presence of God in our own houses of worship makes them also suggestive of the truth that God was made flesh and dwelt among us.

In the doctrine of the sanctuary, as we have thus far beheld it, we have seen no contact of Deity with fallen humanity. In the Temple, His place of manifestation was inaccessible; while in His human nature, Christ, though made like unto His brethren and though tempted in all respects like as we are, was yet without sin. The intercourse which Jesus so fully held with men, while resident on earth, approaches nearest to this contact. It was, however, to be fully exemplified in the indwelling of the Holy Ghost in the individual believer.

It was on the same night in which He was betrayed that, in the comforting discourse delivered by Christ to His disciples, the promise of this indwelling was first given. "If ye love me," said Jesus, "keep my commandments. And I will pray the Father, and he shall give you another Comforter, that he may abide with you for ever; even the Spirit of truth; whom the world cannot receive, because it seeth him not, neither knoweth him: but ye know him; for he dwelleth in you, and shall be with you" (John 14:15-17).

The same doctrine was taught, in a more distinct form, by the apostle, to the Corinthians. "Know ye not," says he, in one part of his Epistle, "that ye are the temple of God, and that the Spirit of God dwelleth in you?" (1 Cor. 3:16). And three chapters afterwards, he repeats the idea: "What? know ye not that your body is the temple of the Holy Ghost which is in you?" (1 Cor. 6:19).

A great gulf has been passed between the doctrine heretofore displayed and the new development which we have here reached. The Holy God, who cannot look upon sin with any degree of allowance, has here brought Himself into contact with those in whom it resides. We may account for it as much as we may, but the removal of our guilt through the atonement of Christ, by the imputed righteousness of Christ; nay, by the whole work, in every form of Him who is made unto us wisdom, righteousness, sanctification, and redemption, we have yet much that is mysterious in this wondrous grace of God. While we may recognize in the sacrifice of the incarnate Savior more evidences of love and grace, neither in that incarnation itself, nor in the former indwelling of God with man, do we see such depth of condescension as in the indwelling of the Holy Ghost.

Well, indeed, might Christ comfort His disciples for the loss of His presence, by the promise of this blessed Comforter; and justly does the apostle suggest that in-dwelling as a reason why we should eschew all defilement of our bodies. The God of holiness dwells within us. The Spirit, whose distinctive name is Holy, has made us His temple. Shall we not the rather seek to make it daily more meet for its heavenly visitor?

How blessed would it be could we ever keep this doctrine in remembrance. The inhabitant within us would find us ever working out our own salvation, knowing that God is working in us both to will and to do according to His good pleasure. Our fellow Christians would be duly regarded. We would recognize in them, also, the temples of the Holy Ghost. And while we learn to love them for the fruits they display, we would be shirking from offending them, from doing them any injury, from exercising toward them any malice for injuries received. Because with all its deformity, we behold a temple of God, sanctified to us by its holy inhabitant. Let this building, my brethren, ever be a monitor of this doctrine, that as you perceive God dwells in it, so also may you recognize His presence in you, begetting holiness, and love, and zeal.

The temple in the individual under another form is now fulfilling, in its last antitype, the prophetic symbolism of the sanctuary. A great temple of

God is now building. The materials began to be gathered in the beginning of the world. They are still gathering. They will not cease to be gathered until the day when the heavens and earth shall pass away. These materials are the saints of God, fitted by the indwelling of the Spirit for this new and glorious habitation of God.

> Now therefore ye are no more strangers and foreigners, but fellow-citizens with the saints, and of the household of God; and are built upon the foundation of the apostles and prophets, Jesus Christ himself being the chief corner stone; in whom all the building fitly framed together groweth into an holy temple in the Lord: in whom also ye are builded together for an habitation of God through the Spirit (Eph. 2:19-22).

"To whom coming, as unto a living stone, disallowed indeed of men, but chosen of God, and precious, ye also, as lively stones, are built up a spiritual house, an holy priesthood, to offer up spiritual sacrifices, acceptable to God by Jesus Christ" (1 Pet. 2:4-5).

> And I saw a new heaven and a new earth: for the first heaven and the first earth were passed away; and there was no more sea. And I John saw the holy city, new Jerusalem, coming down from God out of heaven, prepared as a bride adorned for her husband. And I heard a great voice out of heaven saying, Behold, the tabernacle of God is with men, and he will dwell with them, and they shall be his people, and God himself shall be with them, and be their God (Rev. 21:1-3).

It is here, my brethren, that we begin to see what purposes of His glory God had in view in the manifestations of His grace to men. It is that He may build of such materials as these, an eternal habitation. He wishes to inhabit the praise of Israel. The temple He is creating is one not composed of angelic intelligences, but of sinful men. It is to be one where dwelleth no natural holiness or righteousness, but which is composed of those who ascribe to God all the praise of their salvation. He has taken its materials from the morally polluted. He has redeemed them from their defilement, made them lively and spiritual stones fitted for His spiritual temple, and now He is building them upon His own chosen apostles and prophets, Jesus Himself being the chief corner-stone. Silently are the walls arising. There is neither hammer nor axe, nor any tool of iron heard in the house while it is building. Each stone is fitted for its place by the workmanship of the Spirit; the messengers of God are daily gathering them to their places. The time approaches when the work will be completed, and the King of Zion shall enter to take up His perpetual abode. Lord, hasten the glorious day!

"He which testifieth these things saith, Surely I come quickly. Amen. Even so, come, Lord Jesus" (Rev. 22:20).

Then, then shall be lifted up the true song of dedication. As we remember the grace of God, as each one feels the mighty conflict by which he has been rescued, as the full glory of God bursts upon our vision, the welcome acclamations shall re-sound, "Lift up your heads, O ye gates; and be ye lift up, ye everlasting doors; and the King of glory shall come in. Who is this King of glory? The Lord strong and mighty, the Lord mighty in battle. Who is this King of glory? The Lord of hosts, he is the King of glory" (Ps. 24:7-8, 10).

Then shall be consummated the doctrines and the uses of all God's dwelling places. God grant that we may all be present there! To be shut out from that temple will be to be shut out from the presence of God forever. Let the hopes which it holds forth animate us all to more devotion, more holiness, more trust in Christ, that we may be made meet to be partakers. Meantime, my brethren, as you enter this house, from time to time, sanctify it by these holy associations. Let us dedicate it, indeed, to the worship of God, to the promulgation of His Word and to the administration of His ordinances. Let it be sacred, as His chosen dwelling-place among His people; let it tell of Him who was made flesh and dwelt among us. Let it remind you of the sacred presence of the Spirit in the individual believer. Let it ever bring to view that glorious temple which shall be truly fitted to speak for the praises of God.

For such objects as these, and for such alone, may it stand until that better temple is complete. God preserve it from earthquake and from fire, from the destruction of the tornado, and from the ruthless hand of man. God grant that it may be a blessing to you, to this community, and to the world. May influences ever go forth hence which shall tend to the honor of His name, to the glory of His cause. And as one after another of those now worshiping here shall be removed, as stones fitted by the habitations above, God grant that others may arise, that numerous increase may be given, so that a church holding forth the principles which we regard to be those of God's word may be ever preserved.

To God be all praise, that He has kept you these fifty years past faithful to these principles. To Him be all praise, that in the erection of this building He has the better fitted you to maintain and proclaim them. To Him be all praise, that He sends you this day a pastor to break to you the Bread of life. To Him be all praise, if He shall keep you faithful henceforth, witnessing for His name and laboring for His cause. To Him and to His grace I commend you. May He ever dwell among you, showing forth His glory, teaching His truth, fitting you for His presence, inhabiting your praises here, and preparing for you a habitation in which ye shall dwell forever and forever.

Note

*A sermon preached September 25, 1859, at the dedication of the new house of worship of the Baptist Church at Columbia, South Carolina.

8

Life and Death the Christian's Portion*

Text: For all things are yours; whether Paul, or Apollos, or Cephas, or the world, or life, or death, or things present, or things to come; all are yours (1 Cor. 3:21-22).

The apostle has elsewhere taught us that all things work together for good to them that love God. He here informs us that this cooperation for the welfare of the people of God is so complete that God does not simply bless in the good and overrule in the evil, but gives all things to His servants. It is for the Christian that they exist and to him that they belong. The circumstances that surround him are not simply productive for his welfare, but he has a right of ownership in each of them. It is not incidentally, nor accidentally only, that they contribute to his happiness, but they are distinctly purposed to this end. They are not his in the aggregate merely, so that their prevalent tendency is for his welfare, but each event is a blessing, made such either directly or under the overruling power of God.

Notice the emphatic manner in which our text declares this truth. At the beginning the apostle says, "All things are yours"; at the end he repeats these words. Meanwhile, lest any should think that he does not mean absolutely all things, he enumerates certain particulars under which all others are included. These would be the most probable exceptions, were there any such, and thus Paul plainly evinces that there are none. Not death itself, that last and fearful enemy of man, is excluded from the list; nor even life, otherwise so fleeting in its gifts and pleasures, and realized as to all except the child of God to be such a failure. These, as well as all others, belong to the Christian.

While the general truth thus stated by the apostle is at all times full of consolation, and especially when any of us are passing through periods of deep affliction, the present occasion the rather directs our attention to the specific statements made about death and life. In the dealings of God with our departed brother, we have no common example of the fulfillment of these statements. As introductory to the consideration of that life it may not be unprofitable to contemplate for a while these particular teachings of the text—that life belongs to the Christian, and that death also is his.

I. *Life is the especial portion of the Christian.*

To the world this appears to be far from true. In its most evident aspect the life of the Christian is the same with that of others. No special protection from God, no angelic guidance, no miraculous powers of self-protection manifest a life of peculiar favor. Even where men are disposed to admit a difference because of the presence of divine grace, life is not believed to be a peculiar blessing. On the contrary, it seems more painful than pleasant, something to shake off rather than cling to. It is, indeed, spent in the service of God, but to their eyes this is, to say the least of it, at present in vain. It may bring reward hereafter, but in this world it makes no other change than to add to pain and care. It directs him to control his desires even to the extent of abstinence from pleasures that are innocent. It gives to his conduct new laws, which enjoin meekness and patience under injuries and love and prayer for persecuting enemies. It demands such supreme love that only through deprivation of all things, and relative hatred of the dearest ties, and even of his own life, can he be a worthy disciple of his Master.

Can a life of such deprivation and sacrifice belong to him? With duties so difficult, sufferings so unendurable, and temptations which cannot always be overcome, can it be called an especial portion?

Surely, the apostle must be speaking of the future life, in which God marks more plainly the contrast between the righteous and the wicked; in which the evils of this world are taken away and the happiness of the Christian confirmed forever. To that life such a character may be given, but surely not to this. Yet that it is of this that he is writing is evident from the contrast with death; this life alone is the opposite of the only death that befalls the Christian. It is this, therefore, that he calls the especial property of the Christian.

In confirmation of this declaration, I remark:

1. *That had not God intended life as a blessing He would not have caused the Christian to pass through it.*

The life of pilgrimage on earth is not essential to the Christian. There are many saved who never live it. In the case of infants, it is enough that they live long enough to die. God gives them life in no other respect as their portion. He might deal in like manner with all the saved. But He does not. To others life is not a mere momentary or brief existence, but a course of experience running through a longer or shorter period of time. It was to those who had such life that this epistle was written. It is of such life, therefore, that the apostle says, "It is yours." That life included time spent in the service of God and other time in which they had lived without Him. Yet there is no qualification in the language. The whole life was theirs: that out of Christ, that in Christ; that spent in sin, that in struggles after holiness; all was theirs. Not a moment, not an event is excluded. The days of sin had been operative to make them feel their need of Christ as had been those of holy life to bind more closely to Him. If there be no life subsequent to conversion, as in the case of the penitent thief, there still belongs to the believer the life before that period. Whatever portion God gives, that portion is His. The babe has what he has because just that alone would be a blessing. Why God does not give further life to any of the saved, with whatever blessing it would bring, we know not. God only knows. Perhaps the gift of the temporal stay on earth would deprive of the eternal life, and therefore to these it is not given, because it would not be a blessing.

The blessing too associated with the life depends not upon its being what is called a happy life. It matters not what may be its nature, whether it be spent in joy or in sorrow; in activity for God, or in enforced quietness; whether the soul be brought early or late to the reception of Jesus; whatever the life itself which God gives to the Christian, that life is a blessing and has been given for his assured happiness.

Nor does this arise from any blind and disconnected purpose of God, but from the inseparable connection of secondary causes through which He carries out His will. Because of this the life of the Christian is not measured by the days he spends on earth. Upon that life here, whether brief or long, God has concentrated all things. Toward it come influences from all the past. From it go forth influences to all the future. These are for the most part unseen, unfelt, unrealized, but they have actual existence. Each individual Christian stands in the world, as though for himself alone had God created or ruled the universe or sent forth His Son to redeem. It is not simply all things for all, but all things for each one. All the purposes and acts of God, which respect either the future or the past, are concentrated on each one, as though there were no other. And as was true of the head, so also is it of the members, the central point of that concentration is found in the life here on earth. It is true that such action is beyond the comprehension of the finite—but not beyond the infinite actor.

Whatever, therefore, may be the remoteness of these events, however numerous they are, however multiplied in their efforts and application to different ones of his people, however interwoven the events, God has yet concentrated them so fully upon this one life that it may justly be said all things belong to it. To His eye they are identified with it, though no creature can perceive it. Yet as in the resurrection body the elements, however scattered, will be gathered together to conscious full identity, in like manner when God shall make plain all His works from the beginning to the end, the Christian will perceive the now unseen influences which have bound to this life of his all that has been, is, and shall be. Thus belonging to the life they belong to him that leads it. It is for him, not for his life, that they are thus concentrated. It is through these that God makes him what he is here, and shall be hereafter, and through these that the life here is the precursor of the true life to come. It is thus that to the Christian life is an especial portion.

2. I have thus far been speaking of life as a blessing, without regard to its character. *It is evident, however, that there must be such a thing as true life for a moral and intellectual being.* That life must be based upon conformity to moral law, and the perception of the beauty and glory of the Infinitely Great and Good. It is because the life which God gives the Christian here is of this true character, that it may further be called a blessed portion. By God's grace he is enabled to live a life worthy of an immortal and spiritual being.

By this it is not meant that sin will in no respect be present and exercise no influence. God does not give this perfect life. The life here has its failures and its sins, just as it has its sorrows and its afflictions. Yet it is such a life as becomes an immortal and spiritual being, such as none out of Christ can live, but such as is attained in Him, though in much weakness and with many infirmities.

It is a life in which God is made the chief end of being. To Him are given the best affections of the heart. Obedience to His law is a true delight. Communion with Him is earnestly sought. His rule is acknowledged, and dependence upon Him is a heartfelt joy. It is a life in which is recognized the true nature of the human brotherhood. God is seen in man, as the common Creator, in whose image we have been made. His fellow Christians are linked to him by the common Savior, in whose blood we have been redeemed. The blessings that surround in life awaken gratitude toward the Divine Giver. The sufferings and ills that befall are known as chastisements from a Father's hand. Thus in the surroundings of his life, as well as in its Author and Preserver, does God, and only God, enter into his soul.

It is a life, indeed, of infirmities—but of infirmities from the punishment of which he has been released by the sufferings of Christ and from all the sin of which the blood of Christ has cleansed. They are left that he may struggle against them—that by these godly exercises he may grow up unto the full stature of a man in Christ Jesus. For this purpose grace is bestowed. The Holy Spirit dwells within the heart, sanctifying by its presence and leading on to the perfection, which it is God's purpose that he shall finally attain. There is no danger, therefore, of failure in such a life. The divine power within secures the final result. The eternal purpose of God with respect to it shall assuredly be attained.

If, on this account, however, we should think the Christian to be only the passive recipient of the divine influences, we should greatly mistake the teachings of God's Word. It is not God's purpose to cast every man in the same mold, nor to leave him entirely independent of his own action. Each one is to have individual existence. His life is also to be his own creation. Upon what he does is his growth to depend. He is himself to work out his own salvation. And the position that he shall occupy hereafter is determined by his position here—by the spirituality he attains, the knowledge he acquires, the intimacy of his communion with God, and the spirit of activity and sacrifice he exhibits. God is the worker, but so also is man. The labors of each are necessary, and the extent of this necessity for mutual labor cannot be too strongly stated. Without God, man must perish. Without man, God's work will never be accomplished. Such is the constitution which God has chosen to establish.

It would be vain to say that we can understand why this is so or in what manner it takes place. But the fact is plainly revealed. *God works as though man had nothing to do, and requires man to work as though God had left him to himself.* None but God can thus control and yet leave uncontrolled. But it is God that does it. So also in the imperfect life. God has fixed it all. His purposes extend to every act and word and thought. Yet does man also fix it all; for every act and word and thought is consciously the result of his own will and of the previous acts. God overrules these, as well as extraneous events, to secure the final result; yet so overrules, not by any compulsory action on man, but in accordance with the law of freedom bestowed upon his being. Thus is it that even in this dispensation of all grace, God has provided a place for human efforts, and given to man the opportunity to secure reward. According to his toils and cares, his sufferings and trials, his temptations and struggles, his yearnings after and prayers to God, and in all of these according to the use he makes of such opportunities in life, is the reward which God gives. That reward begins here. It is often bestowed when the recipient knows it not. Even for our most secret services God bestows it openly. But in the world to come, it shall be plainly revealed in all its fullness. There shall the labors of this life secure a greater or less reward, according to their deserts.

The glory and gradations of such a life, we are not able to perceive here on earth. We see not even the beauty of its essential characteristics, supreme love to God and man. We comprehend not the progress that is made in its attainment. We do not realize the differences that it creates. We are not yet elevated sufficiently above the stage of its action. We are but travellers on the road ascending the rugged pathway. Others are struggling with us to attain the lofty summit. So far from knowing their progress, we know little of our own. Much that we have achieved is concealed by the winding path. Ofttimes we are shut up in such darkness as can be felt. We see but a step behind, but a step before. We perceive sometimes that we are descending and begin to doubt if we are on the right road. Occasionally, to cheer us, we are permitted to stop at some point of observation and look below to the depth from which we have come, or above to the summit which we are gradually approaching.

But for the most part we have to go forward, in faith, that He who has made our path has made it as shall best enable us finally to attain. But, while thus we journey, there is One who sits above, who marks every step. At every moment He can tell where we are, and how we are progressing, and what are our needs. It is His hand that holds forth to us the prize; His voice of cheer that encourages us to press on; His magic power that invigorates our wearied limbs, or makes firm our tottering steps. It is because of Him that such a journey is possible. It is He that greets every one with the plaudit, "Well done," as he emerges from the strain and toil, covered though he be with the earth-stains of his slips and falls.

The Christian arrives at his heavenly home, humbled because of his life, glorying only in Christ. He knows that he has no merit. He feels that, with his best efforts, he is but unprofitable. He is ready to ascribe all to God. The life he has lived he feels to be too unworthy of the grace he has received. The language of his heart is, "I am not worthy to be called Thy son." But he finds the countenance of his Savior filled with joy, because of the life, which the soul crucified with Him and in whom He has lived, has been able to live in the flesh by the faith of the Son of God. He learns how God had made him his co-worker to this end; and as he looks back upon the life he has achieved, he perceives how truly that life has been to him a blessed portion bestowed by God.

3. All that I have thus far said would be true, however, if into that world above nothing but the result of this life were taken. The blessing then would consist only in the increased power and position, derived from the life on earth. This increase alone would be the advantage over the life which would have been his, had he died in infancy. *But this life is also seen to be the portion of the Christian, from the fact that he carries it with him in all its entireness into the external world.* Not a particle of it is left behind. Much of it, that had been forgotten here on earth, is again present with him. Its

fullness, as comprising all things, is now revealed to him. And it becomes a possession to be eternally present.

The Scriptures tell us that the life itself is the privilege; and they explain the fact by teaching us that at death we enter not upon the new life, stripped of the things which belong to us here, but that we carry our past life with us, to be made a constituent part of that we are about to enjoy. The works of the Christian follow him into heaven. He has made friends to himself of the things of this world and is, therefore, received into heavenly habitations. The gradations of that world are fixed, in part if not entirely, by the scenes of this. That life which, when he was on earth, was hid with Christ in God, is now in his possession.

His crown is now studded with the stars placed there by his earthly labors. The garments which clothe him have been whitened by the blood of Christ, but they also mark the tribulations through which he has passed. The palms in his hand speak of the victories he had achieved. With all others, he casts all that he is and has at the feet of the Lamb, acknowledging that he has been rescued and purified and glorified only by His blood and His power and His grace. Yet it is in that life of earth thus translated to the skies that he is able to comprehend with all saints what is the breadth and length and depth and height of the love of Christ. For in it he sees himself a monument of grace, erected as a pillar in the house of God, to His infinite praise and glory.

To know God as fully as mortal can know, he must only know himself. The conviction of personal nothingness in the eyes of God may have him cry out in this world. "What is man, that thou art mindful of him?" But the contemplation of that life which is now fully his, and of the skill and power and goodness with which God has wrought it out, will make him now exclaim,

> I will praise thee; for I am fearfully and wonderfully made: marvellous are thy works; and that my soul knoweth right well. My substance was not hid from thee, when I was made in secret, and curiously wrought in the lowest parts of the earth. Thine eyes did see my substance, yet being unperfect; and in thy book all my members were written, which in continuance were fashioned, when as yet there was none of them. How precious also are thy thoughts unto me, O God! how great is the sum of them! If I should count them, they are more in number than the sand: when I awake, I am still with Thee (Ps. 139:14-18).

These words are true, not simply of the natural life, but also of the spiritual. Thus has God ever viewed it from His eternal standpoint. Thus does man behold it, when eternity opens his eyes to its true nature. And then is it that he knows what is the meaning of the apostle's saying, "Life is yours." It is not simply as God's gift, nor as a blessing in itself though confined to earth, nor as a capacity for a true moral and spiritual elevation in the life to come; but it is his as carried item by item into that life, entering into all its fullness, inseparably connected with it, and furnishing the food for the contemplation and joy of God throughout eternity. Surely such life is a blessing.

If but brief, yet blessed in its relations to the past and future; yet more blessed if protracted. Blessed if spent most feebly because still entering thus into the joys of eternity—but blessed beyond all thought if so used here that it carried with it into the eternal world the rich rewards of faith and active piety. Well might the aged man of God who lies before us, after giving to the service of Christ a life continued from youth to the days of a ripe old age, exclaim, even here on earth, in the calm contemplation of his life, "I have not found, nor do I consider it true that life was a failure. Taking up Jesus as the aim of life, there is sufficient to support a man, and life is a reality indeed, and not a failure. I would be willing, with Him, to live life over."

This is not the language of the worldly man clinging to time, and fearful that the ties be cut; but of one who had looked on a life lived with Jesus in the light of the Word of God and to whom, in the days of his quiet waiting for his change, God had shown his entire possession of the life of this world as well as of the next. To attain the knowledge of this truth, as a part of the Word of God, is not so difficult. To make a personal application of it is what few are able to do in this life. God granted this privilege to our departed brother. Yet to him there was little known here compared with that knowledge he has now acquired. Into that fruition the imagination of man cannot follow him. The language of the lips would be inadequate to express it. But blessed be God, He assures us that even the imperfect lives, which we are now living on earth, are such as He has thus associated with the joys of heaven. And though we be now too unworthy to see here what God has wrought out in the life He has given, and too incapacitated to perceive, that life here with Christ is no failure; yet in the world above, even to our weakness, shall be granted that higher knowledge which our brother now possesses.

Whatever circumstances in this life seem at present to cast doubt upon the fact will then be explained. It may be that, in those most adverse, will be recognized the chief agencies used by God to make this life a blessing. But whether this prove true or not, the revelation God shall make of His dealings with his people will show that, to each one of the multitude of the saved the life on earth has been, and will ever continue to be, a blessed portion.

II. *We turn now to the other declaration of the apostle that death also belongs to the Christian.*

This seems less probable than that life should be his. Life is of the nature of a blessing and only rendered otherwise by sin. Death has been a curse from the beginning. That it should become otherwise seems contrary to its very nature. And yet, such is the emphatic declaration of the apostle. Life is yours. But death also is yours. God gives you a right of possession in it. You shall make it for your happiness. So, also, will He.

But how is it made so? Not by escaping it. For the Christian also is mortal. Not by its assuming a pleasant aspect. For the Christian shrinks from its loathsome embrace. It is not the sinful nature alone that dreads it. The renewed nature, yea, even the perfect nature, holds back from contact with it. The Scripture, speaking of the destruction of death, still calls it the last enemy. It remains still an enemy, though a conquered one, and one used by the Conqueror for the benefit of his people.

It is well that this fact should be borne in mind. To many it seems strange, that one with the Christian's hopes and consolations should cling to life, or fear the embrace of death. But God has not left us simply to pass through death as an event, but also to recognize it as an enemy, and to endure it as such. He has had a purpose in this, and that purpose includes the blessing. When that purpose has been fulfilled, the dread of death is dissipated. This sometimes occurs before, but most frequently at the hour of death; so that even the most timid Christian is so supported at that solemn time that he calmly falls into its embrace, as one sinks into a gentle slumber. But it suits not God often to anticipate in the ordinary life the grace which overcomes in the dying moment. Did He choose to do so, it would be manifest to all that death is ours. But while this is not done, He makes that fact equally plain to those who will study His acts, by the course through which He subjects us to it.

1. *He makes it ours because by its contemplation He draws the soul away from this world and ripens it for heaven.*

The life which God permits to us is short. The Scriptures press this fact upon our attention. Our days are few and swiftly pass away.

Brief, too, as these lives are, God makes them still more so by the uncertainty with which He keeps death ever present as a possibility. As the vitality of the church is quickened by the uncertain period of the return of her Lord, so that of the Christian is equally secured by his ignorance of the moment when he shall be summoned to meet Him.

It is remarkable to what an extent the Word of God urges the prospect of death upon us. It is not to the sinner alone that it is held up, but to the Christian also. Scarcely, indeed, can one look into any portion of his Christian life that he does not see death summoned for the purpose of its illustration. The sin committed in Adam has brought death. Regeneration consists in the quickening into life of those dead in trespasses and sins. The law, as a covenant, cannot be kept, and by the grace of Christ he must become dead to it. His union to Christ under the new covenant is marked by crucifixion to the world. His public profession of His name sets forth His death to sin and resurrection to a new life, inasmuch as he has been baptized into the death of Christ, and, therefore, buried with Him by baptism into death, that he might be with Him a partaker of the resurrection from the dead. The remnants of sin are the body of death, from which he prays deliverance. While the very feast of the church, its most blessed privilege, invites, whenever spread, to meditation upon the death of Christ, the foundation of all the Christian's hope, the source of his real life.

What does all this mean? It is from God. It therefore indicates a purpose. *It shows that this contemplation of death is one of the most potent means of advancing the Christian's life and securing his happiness.* It is thus that we are led never to forget that we are pilgrims and strangers, who have no abiding city, and hence are induced to seek the citizenship that is in heaven. It is thus that eternity is kept ever before us, that in the remembrance of it we may be diligent in the earthly kingdom of our Lord. It is thus that amid our trials and sufferings we may be consoled by their short duration. It is thus that amid persecutions for righteousness' sake we should not forget the future Judge that will avenge, yea, even the Savior that endured. It is thus that sin is restrained by the beatific visions that are called to mind. It is thus that the ties that bind to earth are broken, and the affections are set on Christ above. It is thus that the soul is taught to yearn for that life into which shall come no sorrow, and which shall have no end in death. It is thus that God alone is felt to be the satisfying portion of the soul.

What is it that the Scripture teaches by these facts, but that for the best welfare of the Christian death must be contemplated not only as an event of life, but as one that may happen at any time? It does not assert that the endurance of death is essential, or is a blessing in itself—on the contrary, it speaks of many who shall not pass through it. At least two of the human race have already escaped the contest. It is the expectation of death, therefore, not the actual experience of it, that is necessary to the best interest of the Christian. To secure such blessings as God would give, death must be the usual lot, and the apprehension of it, must be universal.

It is through this apprehension that God constantly brings His children more closely to Himself—and thus makes death a blessing to all, even to those who escape actual contact with it.

2. *Death further belongs to the Christian, because its sting has been removed in the removal of sin.* It is because this is only partially realized, that death can at any time alarm the Christian. He may shrink from it, but he is not afraid of it. Whenever fear is realized, it is because of teachings of God's Word are not sufficiently known or because of the imperfection of life, which causes him to doubt his actual connection with Christ. God may permit this at other times, but when death is near, so clearly does the Spirit reveal His truth, and so fully does the Savior bear up even the weakest lamb of the flock, that all terror departs.

But it is the Christian's privilege at all times to realize the removal of sin. Its penalty has been borne by his Almighty Savior. The justice of God no longer demands his death. The wrath of God has been forever averted. The demands of the law have been completely fulfilled. By a perfect union with Jesus by faith all these blessings have been made his. He is, therefore, no longer to be treated as a sinner, but accepted in the Beloved Son. The honor and truth of the Godhead are pledged for his everlasting happiness. His transgressions have been removed far from him, and in the removal of sin the sting of death has been taken away.

It is true that sin has not been entirely eradicated. It is left that he may be made more diligent and watchful and may feel more fully his dependence on Christ. A true view of God's dealings teaches him that this fearful plague is overruled to his greater good. But this is not all his comfort. He has already discovered that with all its power it has lost dominion over him. Through the grace of God he finds that he can obtain the mastery. Through faith in the Son of God he can come off more than conqueror. Its presence has no power to dismay, because he knows that He who has torn up the root can in his own time remove or destroy the dying fibers left still clinging to the soil.

The author of our text himself gives us a leaf from his own experience in striking confirmation of this truth. Behold the struggles of his inner life recorded in the seventh chapter of Romans—and mark how, even when brought, as one would imagine, to the depths of despair, crying out, "O wretched man that I am! who shall deliver?" his faith fails not, but with triumphant joy he exclaims, "I thank God through Jesus Christ our Lord."

Turn also, in connection, to that place in First Corinthians, where he has announced that flesh and blood cannot inherit the kingdom of God and is enforcing the necessity either of death or of something equivalent, and learn how this Christian who cried out for deliverance from sin can view the hour of dissolution or change.

> Behold, I show you a mystery; We shall not all sleep, but we shall all be changed, in a moment, in the twinkling of an eye, at the last trump: for the trumpet shall sound, and the dead shall be raised incorruptible, and we shall be changed. For this corruptible must put on incorruption, and this mortal must put on immortality. So when this corruptible shall have put on incorruption, and this mortal shall have put on immortality, then shall be brought to pass the saying that is written, Death is swallowed up in victory. O death, where is thy sting? O grave, where is thy victory? The sting of death is sin; and the strength of sin is the law. But thanks be to God, which giveth us the victory through our Lord Jesus Christ (1 Cor. 15:51-57).

What but such a mastery as this can rob the king of terrors of his power? Without the revelation of such hope, with what unspeakable agony must man approach the hour of dissolution! The period of God's longer forbearance is about to expire. The curse of sin is now to be realized. Its impress upon him, and its power over him, are now to be made eternal. His final destiny is now to be fixed. The nature of the eternal world is now opening upon his sight. It is sin that has brought him to this moment of agony. That sin cannot now be shaken off. The power with which it grasps has grown into his very life, and with that life is forever to be indissolubly bound. Its exceeding sinfulness is now perceived. The terrors of God are gathering around his soul. The scorching fires of His wrath are beginning to be felt. The stings of conscience are piercing him like a sword. He sees the folly of the past, the vanity of his life, his utter want of excuse before God, and he cannot meet him. The sting remains. It has not been removed. Death must be met with its full terrors. And the wretched soul prays but for a moment's continuance, even of this miserable life, rather than yield to the dreaded embrace of his conquering foe.

What a contrast this to the death of the Christian!—a contrast, too, that would be deepened, could eternity be truly revealed to each. The lost soul but begins to know the horrors that threaten him. The Christian but faintly perceives the joys that await him.

His faith in the presence of his Savior is still feeble. His knowledge of his relation to God still imperfect, while it is only in the experience beyond death that he shall know the blessed nature of his immortality.

Yet even under these imperfect influences, so great is the contrast that the ownership of death by the Christian is manifest. The sting has been taken away. Death is now no longer dreaded—some even welcome it with exultant joy; others only await it with calm but ready acquiescence in the will of God; but it is met by all with the firm conviction, that it is a conquered foe, which has no longer power but to bless.

If then death no otherwise affected the Christian's happiness than to draw to God in life, and to be confidently met at its approach, it might well be called his portion.

3. *But it is also his, because it is the portal to eternal life.*

I am not unmindful of the instances we have already seen where eternal life is otherwise attained. But as I then suggested that death as contemplated was essentially present, so also even those who do not pass through what is commonly known as death experience a change which has, so far as the present consideration is concerned, all its essential requisites. The world and all that has belonged to earthly existence has passed away. Heaven with all its joys is appearing and the position of bliss into which the child of God is brought is confirmed eternally. It is because death secures these to all to whom it comes, that it is the portion of the Christian.

The teaching of the Scripture is not simply to continued existence, even in a happy state, but of an enduring existence confirmed in happiness and true holiness. This is the life and immortality which Christ has brought to light.

Even for the knowledge of continued life we are indebted to the Word of God. With all the suggestions of the mind, filled with longings for life, and refusing to believe in the annihilation of the soul—with all the guidance of God's teachings in the past handed down through the traditions common to all men—the wisest philosophers, seeking most earnestly after proofs, have been unable to produce them. So little does man know, that even the greatest minds, so far from discovering this truth, have been unable to illustrate it when revealed, and to build it up by arguments satisfactory even to themselves. God alone has taught it, and the proof of it is to be found only in such teaching of God. The fact itself arises only because He has chosen to establish such continuity to spiritual life.

He who will thoughtfully consider this subject must be convinced, that our spirits continue beyond death because God so wills it; and that He has given no distinct declaration that He so wills, except in His written revelation. There He teaches us that death does not destroy the spirit, but simply separates it for a time from the body, with which in due time it shall again be reunited.

It is not as it leads only to an immortality such as this, however, that death is ours. Into that continued state go the spirits, not of the righteous only, but of the wicked also—yet the righteous only "hath hope in his death; the wicked is driven away in his wickedness." Such immortality is to the latter the most fearful evil. The death that leads to it has taken away all hope of change because it has terminated that stay on earth, during which alone salvation may be secured. That determination has fixed forever his destiny of woe. Death is to him the servant of divine justice, inflicting that most fearful penalty of sin, a never ending existence, destroyed in all its true life by the presence of that evil which the sinner has voluntarily chosen, and in which in this world he has striven to find delight.

The continued existence of the Christian, however, is one of bliss. His sins have been removed, and he passes into the heavenly world to enjoy a condition of complete purity and happiness. Not only thus, but that condition is a confirmed one. As the wicked shall not change his state so shall not the righteous his. The day of his trial and probation is over—and he stands secure of the bliss of heaven confirmed by the unfailing promises of God. The scenes, through which he has passed on earth, fill him with no apprehensions that his weakness and insufficiency will disable him from performing the perfect service of heaven. The recollection of Adam's trial will suggest to him no possibility that he will be subjected to a test which will dissolve forever the bands which unite him to God. Even the sin of the angels will not alarm him. For he is now possessed of that "eternal life, which God, that cannot lie, promised before the world began."

His destiny is as fixed in God's grace and in His truth, as are the foundations of the eternal throne. That promise of God is enough; His grace can never be exhausted. His truth can never fail. Were the Christian ignorant of the facts on which that promise is based, still the promise is enough. But God has laid bare the glorious foundation of our hope. It is in the incarnate Word—in the glorious person and work of Christ. He it is, with whom an eternal covenant was made. He it is, who as the representative of His people, has fulfilled the covenant. He it is, who as alone God and man had laid hold upon both God and man, and reconciled them to each other. The sacrifice needed for this work was infinite, but has been made by Him who being God hath given to the sufferings in His human nature a divine value and efficacy. The infinite demands of justice have thus been met. The probation once for all has been stood. The demands of the covenant have been fulfilled. And God has promised that He shall see of the travail of His soul and shall be satisfied.

The covenant thus made was eternal and does not terminate in time. The satisfaction thus rendered was infinite and cannot be exhausted. The travail thus endured was priceless, and its recompense can never end. And thus is it that eternal life is secured to the people of God. He shall dwell forever with God, the self-existent, and absolutely eternal because it is this God that has thus entered into his life and imparted to it an assured and coeternal immortality.

This, this is immortality indeed, and it is to such immortality that God makes death the portal. What power then has death except to serve? What pain can it inflict? Of what blessings can it deprive for which it makes not ample compensations? Nay how can these things be weighed against each other? It is to put in the scales the small dust of the balance, as opposed to the weight of worlds. It is to compare the finite with the infinite, a moment of time with eternity, and the merely human with that into which the divine so largely enters. As it certainly leads to such glory, death can be no otherwise regarded than as the servant of the Christian.

4. I remark finally that *death belongs to the Christian, because he is permitted to use it to give testimony to Christ.*

It is a privilege to testify of what we know—a still greater one if our testimony be of important facts, the knowledge of which will benefit or honor the one we love. Especially is this felt if our opportunity to testify be brief, and if it be surrounded by such circumstances as will give it peculiar weight.

Dying testimony is considered especially important. The witness is about to pass into the presence of God; and if his truthfulness can at no other time be relied on, surely it can be then. So fully is this recognized that earthly courts receive a statement given at the moment of death as of higher value than testimony taken under the solemnities of an oath.

It is because of these facts that peculiar interest has always been attached to the dying words and acts of men in religious matters. It is by these that their sincere conviction of the truth of their opinions is tested. Thus may we prove the vanity of infidelity, thus tear the mask from imposture, and thus testify to the power of true religion.

It is the boast of Christianity that it can stand this test in whatever way applied. From the death of Jesus it presents testimony, which may well awaken gratitude and praise to God and confidence and trust in His Son.

But not to our Leader only, but to His followers also, is given this privilege.

Scarcely had the triumphal march of His kingdom begun before one was called into martyrdom to testify not only of his belief in the truth but also of the manifested presence of Christ and His elevation on high. The apostles also sealed this faith with their lives. Even he who had been as one born out of due time, and whose witness in the other respects had extended over most of the then known world, was not exempted.

The same privilege was given to other Christians of that time. They were not allowed, with any fanatical zeal to seek for such a death, but grace was given to meet it when it came. And through it they gave most incontrovertible evidence of the power of the new religion. "The blood of the martyrs became the seed of the Church." Men recognized an unknown power and perceived that nought but supernatural influences could thus lead men even unto death for the sake of a crucified man. Nor was this confined to the apostolic age. Miracles ceased, and prophecies ceased; the days of visions and revelations passed away; but Christ left Himself not without the testimony of martyrs.

It is not permitted to all the servants of Christ to wear the crown of martyrdom, but it is given to all to testify of Him in death. The testimony is no less strong, though it may not be so striking. Around that bed are gathered solemn circumstances. The soul that lies there had professed to serve an invisible Master. Has He a real existence? He professes to have found through Him forgiveness of sins. Has the profession been a true one? He claims to have been supported by Him in many trials of life. Is He able to give support now in this final hour? This Savior has gone before to provide a home for His humble followers. Is he willing with such hope to leave the world? He has been promised His presence, especially in this dark hour. Is it true that Christ is walking with His saint through the valley of the shadow of death, supporting him by His rod and staff, preparing for him a table in the presence of his enemies?

Does anyone doubt that this is so? The Savior invites him to the deathbed of His saints. He selects not for exhibition the one most eminent in piety, nor him who has been most active in benevolence, nor him to whose worthiness the world would most readily testify. Oftentimes He refuses the world the testimony of these. It is not this that is wanted. But He invites to the deathbed of anyone of His people—even the weakest saint may give best testimony to Christ. How from such an one, in such an hour, have been scattered the fears or the frivolities or the over-anxious cares, which have tarnished the Christian life and made it less powerful in its testimony for Jesus! And now hear his testimony against the things which have beclouded that life. It is not the testimony of one who expects punishment and who, to avert it, laments the sin he can no longer repeat. Confidence in Jesus is unshaken. The present Savior is felt and magnified. The lamentation is only about the unworthy use to which the privileges of this world have been put.

And if life is desired, it is only that some reparation may be made to the cause of Christ for past neglects. Yet, even now, the privilege is seized to give in death for Jesus the witness not given in life. What glory does Christ here receive! All that is due to His grace—that grace which so abounds to those that trust Him, that He breaks not the bruised reed and quenches not the smoking flax.

Thus Christ appears not to need the Christian of great acquirements. He can glorify Himself with any of the pupils He has taught. He needs not to take one who has become most skilled or best informed, that He may show forth His praise. He does it in every one—more in one than in another—yet He so does it in all, that all testify of Him, whom not having seen they have believed.

Let the scoffing world account for the universality of such testimony. Were it seen only in the best, it might be thought the result of virtue. Were it only in the wisest, it might be attributed to philosophy. Were it only in the bravest, it might be ascribed to courage. Were it only in the strongest, it might be said to be endurance. Were it only in the most faithful, it might be said to be habit. But when it is seen in those without any of these advantages, but afflicted with their very contraries, to what can it be ascribed but to grace, the grace given by Christ, through whom strengthening the weakest can do all things?

"Precious in the sight of the Lord," says the psalmist, "is the death of his saints." Precious, too, is that scene of the saint himself. It is his great witnessing hour for Jesus when the angels surrounded him to hear the mortal of sense and time testify to the knowledge he has of his invisible Lord and when those of earth who love and trust him most, and among whom his memory is to be embalmed as blessed, are most ready to believe his testimony for Christ and to receive his exhortation to seek salvation in Him. It is well that in such an hour should be shown the power of a religion, which, entering into the wants of our inner nature, testifies even in its feeblest recipient of the ability of God to raise him to a glorious immortality. It is well that, from such witnessing no one should be excluded, on account of such feebleness. It is well that God's power should thus be displayed in such as while testifying for Jesus confess that they themselves are less than the least of all saints. It is well, too, as the records of their lives show that the most eminent servants of God, and His most faithful laborers should declare when dying that they know that their salvation is due to the blood of Jesus and to His grace alone. Thus testifying in one form or another, every Christian is seen in that dread hour of death to be a witness for Jesus. In this respect also, then, is death his.

Note

*Funeral sermon for Basil Manly, Sr.

Bibliography

A. Primary Sources

Boyce, James Petrigru. *Abstract of Systematic Theology.* Philadelphia: American Baptist Publication Society, 1887.

_____. *A Brief Catechism of Bible Doctrine.* Rev. ed. Louisville, Ken.: Coperton and Cotes, 1878.

_____. "The Doctrine of the Suffering Christ." *The Baptist Quarterly* 4 (1870), 385-411.

_____. "The Good Cause." *Louisville Courier Journal,* 3 September 1877. Introductory lecture given on the opening of The Southern Baptist Theological Seminary in Louisville.

_____. *Life and Death the Christian's Portion.* New York: Sheldon and Company, 1869.

_____. Sermon Manuscripts of James Petrigru Boyce. Southern Baptist Theological Seminary Library, Louisville, Kentucky.

_____. *Three Changes in Theological Institutions: An Inaugural Address Delivered before the Board of Trustees of the Furman University:* Greenville, S.C.: C. J. Elford, 1856.

_____. *The Uses and Doctrine of the Sanctuary.* Columbia, S.C.: Robert M. Stokes, 1859.

B. Secondary Sources

Broadus, John A. *Memoir of James Petrigru Boyce.* New York: A. C. Armstrong, 1893.

Cody, Z. T. "James Petrigru Boyce." *Review and Expositor,* 24 (1927), 145-166.

George, Timothy. Review of *Abstract of Systematic Theology* by James Petrigru Boyce. *Review and Expositor,* 81 (1984), 461-464.

_____. "Systematic Theology at Southern Seminary." *Review and Expositor,* 82 (1985), 31-47.

Hinson, E. Glenn. "Between Two Worlds: Southern Seminary, Southern Baptists, and American Theological Education." *Baptist History and Heritage,* 20 (April, 1985), 28-35.

Honeycutt, Roy Lee. "Heritage Creating Hope: The Pilgrimage of The Southern Baptist Theological Seminary." *Review and Expositor,* 81 (1984), 367-391.

Mueller, William A. *A History of Southern Baptist Theological Seminary.* Nashville: Broadman Press, 1959.

Nettles, Thomas J. *By His Grace and For His Glory: A Historical, Theological, and Practical Study of the Doctrines of Grace in Baptist Life.* Grand Rapids: Baker Book House, 1986.

Ramsay, David Marshall. "James Petrigru Boyce, God's Gentleman." *Review and Expositor,* 21 (1924), 129-145.

Sampey, John R. *Southern Baptist Theological Seminary: The First Thirty Years, 1859-1889.* Baltimore: Wharton, Barron & Co., 1890.